Wisdom

Wisdom

Des MacHale

Rupa & Co

First Published 2002 by
Prion Books Limited

First in Rupa Paperback 2003

Published by
Rupa . Co
7/16, Ansari Road, Daryaganj,
New Delhi 110 002

Sales Centres:

Allahabad Bangalore Chandigarh Chennai
Dehradun Hyderabad Jaipur Kathmandu
Kolkata Ludhiana Mumbai Pune

Cover design by Carroll Associates

By arrangement with
Prion Books Limited

This edition is for sale in the Indian sub-continent

ISBN 1-85375-488-9

Printed in India by
Gopsons Papers Ltd.
A-14 Sector 60
Noida 201 301

CONTENTS

INTRODUCTION

While collecting material for a series of books of humorous quotations called *Wit*, I came across a great number of quotations that were profound and meaningful rather than funny. They were the sort of thing that startled you, that hit the spot, that made you sit up and take notice, and of course that made you want to share them with as many other people as possible. It takes an immense amount of skill and verbal expertise to distil a telling truth, a penetrating observation, a heartfelt sermon, a personal philosophy or a whole system of belief into twenty words or less, but that is what all of the people quoted in this book have managed to do.

How should one describe these quotations? They are spiritual in the widest possible sense of the word. This does not mean that the quotations are necessarily religious, though religion has by no means been excluded. I do not always agree with the sentiments expressed (though I often do) and I am sure that neither will every reader, but they are well put, clever and deserve a hearing.

I do not know that I can even begin to define 'wisdom'. We are wise when we put sound knowledge into practice, when we realise the beauty and profundity of our fellow human beings, and when we temper our behaviour with humanity and feeling.

When taking medication of any sort we are

often instructed to take three doses per day – one in the morning, one in the afternoon and one in the evening. May I exhort the reader to partake of this book in the same way? Take three quotes each day and contemplate these and these only, and see how much their wisdom changes your everyday life. The book will thus last you many years (excellent value!) and when you have finished you can start all over again, because by then you will be a different person! The collected wisdom of the ages, from the ancient Greek philosophers right down to present-day sages will then have medicated your body, mind and spirit. I can guarantee that there will be no unpleasant side effects, and who knows, you may even want to pass your newly acquired wisdom on to others.

Des MacHale, 2002

Life and Death

The real test of golf – and life – is not keeping out of the rough, but getting out after we are in.

Henry Lash

Death is the dark backing a mirror needs if we are to see anything.

Saul Bellow

Problems are just opportunities in their work clothes.

Henry J. Kaiser

One dies only once and then for such a long time.

Molière

We are all of us sentenced to solitary confinement inside our own skins, for life.

Tennessee Williams

Any very great and sudden change is death.

Samuel Butler

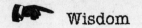

Anyone who wants to make a living folding parachutes ought to be required to jump frequently.

George A. Michael

Death is like the rumble of distant thunder at a picnic.

W. H. Auden

There is no conclusive evidence of life after death. But there is no evidence of any sort against it. You will know soon enough – why worry about it?

John Marshall

A long illness between life and death makes death a comfort both to those who die and to those who remain.

Jean de La Fontaine

Hemingway shot himself. I don't like a man that takes the short way home.

William Faulkner

Death – why this fuss about death? Use your imagination, try to visualise a world without death! Death is an essential condition of life, not an evil.

Charlotte Gilman

It is easier to betray than to remain loyal. It takes far less courage to kill yourself than it takes to make yourself wake up one more time. It's harder to stay where you are than to get out.

Judith Rossner

Death by drunken driving is a socially acceptable form of homicide.

Candy Lightner

There will be no major solution to the suffering of mankind until we reach some understanding of who we are, what the purpose of creation was, what happens after death. Until these questions are resolved, we are caught.

Woody Allen

Why do we kill people who are killing people to show that killing people is wrong?

Holly Near

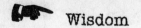

There is no such thing as a death sentence; it is merely a sentence to spend the last days of life as unpleasantly as possible.

Peter Ustinov

We don't know life: how can we know death?

Confucius

While I thought I was learning how to live, I have been learning how to die.

Leonardo da Vinci

Finality is death. Perfection is finality. Nothing is perfect. There are lumps in it.

James Stephens

Death is an acquired trait.

E. Lax

The fear of death is more to be dreaded than death itself.

Publilius Syrus

Sleep is the brother of death.

Homer

Death is not an event in life; we do not experience death.

Ludwig Wittgenstein

I think I am beginning to understand something of it. *(Last words.)*

Auguste Renoir

Money is a singular thing. It ranks with love as man's greatest source of joy. And with his death as his greatest source of anxiety.

J. K. Galbraith

War is death's feast.

George Herbert

Life is a great surprise. I do not see why death should not be an even greater one.

Vladimir Nabokov

All say 'How hard it is that we have to die' – a strange complaint to come from the mouths of people who have had to live.

Mark Twain

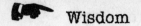

One short sleep past, we wake eternally,
And death shall be no more; Death thou shalt die.

John Donne

Life does not cease to be funny when people die
any more than it ceases to be serious when people
laugh.

George Bernard Shaw

You live only once. But if you work it right, once
is enough.

Anon

How alike are the groans of love to those of the
dying.

Malcolm Lowry

Life is like a very short visit to a toyshop between
birth and death.

Desmond Morris

He who fears death dies every time he thinks of it.

Stanislaus Leszczynski

Life and Death

We are all serving a life sentence in the dungeon
of life.

Cyril Connolly

We should live as if we were never going to die,
for it is the deaths of our friends that hurt us, not
our own.

Gerald Brenan

If you live right, death is a joke to you as far as fear
is concerned.

Will Rogers

The mark of the immature man is that he wants to
die nobly for a cause, while the mark of the
mature man is that he wants to live humbly for
one.

Wilhelm Stekel

Life is a tragedy when seen in close-up and a
comedy in long-shot.

Charlie Chaplin

Suicide is an act of narcissistic manipulation and
deep hostility.

Germaine Greer

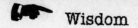

We hear war called murder. It is not: it is suicide.

Ramsay MacDonald

Fish die belly upward and rise to the surface; it is their way of falling.

André Gide

Eternity is not something that begins after you are dead. It is going on all the time. We are in it now.

Charlotte Gilman

Nearly all men die of their medicines and not of their illnesses.

Molière

Of all escape mechanisms, death is the most efficient.

H. L. Mencken

Death is not the greatest loss in life. The greatest loss is what dies inside us while we live.

Norman Cousins

One should always have one's boots on and be ready to leave.

Michel de Montaigne

Life is a flower of which love is the honey.

Victor Hugo

I've had an unhappy life, thank God.

Russell Baker

I believe in the life to come. Mine was always that.

Samuel Beckett

The person by far the most likely to kill you is yourself.

Jock Young

All you can hold in your cold dead hand is what you have given away.

Joaquin Miller

There was never yet an uninteresting life. Such a thing is an impossibility. Inside of the dullest exterior there is a drama, a comedy, and a tragedy.

Mark Twain

Everybody has got to die, but I have always believed an exception would be made in my case.

William Saroyan

What is murder in the first degree? It is the cruel, calculated, cold-blooded killing of a fellow human being. It is the most wicked of crimes and the State is guilty of it every time it executes a human being.

William Randolph Hearst

Strength or weakness at the hour of death depends on the nature of the final illness.

Vauvenargues

For the unhappy man, death is the commutation of a sentence of life imprisonment.

Alexander Chase

We are all of us resigned to death: it's life we aren't resigned to.

Graham Greene

The man who has accomplished all that he thinks worthwhile, has begun to die.

E. T. Trigg

The body of a sensualist is the coffin of a dead soul.

Christian Bovee

Death is part of this life and not of the next.

Elizabeth Bibesco

Neither death nor the sun can be looked at full in the face.

La Rochefoucauld

I am the founder of the Samaritans. I am the only man in the world who cannot commit suicide.

Robert Southey

Put off until tomorrow only what you are willing to die having left undone.

Pablo Picasso

Study as if you were going to live for ever; live as if you were going to die tomorrow.

Maria Mitchell

I have completed an extensive survey on death and have come to just one conclusive conclusion – one out of one dies.

George Bernard Shaw

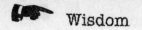

Immortality is a fate worse than death.

Edgar Shoaff

At the funeral of our relations we do our best to put on long faces, but at the luncheon afterwards our hilarity breaks out. For it is he who has died and not ourselves.

Gerald Brenan

In every parting there is an image of death.

George Eliot

All this talk about equality. The only thing people really have in common is that they are all going to die.

Bob Dylan

The opposite of anxiety is not happiness. The opposite of anxiety is death.

Susan Ohanian

The fever called 'Living' is conquered at last.

Edgar Allen Poe

There is but one easy place in this world, and that is the grave.

Henry Ward Beecher

All existence is a theft paid for by other existences; no life flowers except on a cemetery.

Rémy de Gourmont

Anybody who's never watched somebody die is suffering from a pretty bad case of virginity.

John Osborne

Why do the dying never shed tears?

Max Frisch

The bitterest tears shed over graves are for words left unsaid and deeds left undone.

Harriet Beecher Stowe

Never forget that only dead fish swim with the stream.

Malcolm Muggeridge

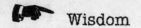

Death is for many of us the gate of hell; but we are inside on the way out, not outside on the way in.

George Bernard Shaw

We sometimes congratulate ourselves at the moment of waking from a troubled dream; it may be so the moment after death.

Nathaniel Hawthorne

Don't be afraid of death. Everyone does it.

Des MacHale

Life is like a game of cards. The hand you are dealt is determinism; the way you play it is free will.

Jawaharlal Nehru

The thought of my sons carrying on after I'm gone is about as close to belief in an afterlife as an ageing pagan like myself is likely to get. But curiously, it's close enough for comfort.

Carey Winfrey

If there wasn't death, I think you couldn't go on.

Stevie Smith

Life and Death

There are two ways to live your life. One is as though nothing is a miracle. The other is as though everything is a miracle.

Albert Einstein

Not a shred of evidence exists in favour of the idea that life is serious.

Brendan Gill

Life is like a B-grade movie. You don't want to leave in the middle of it, but you don't want to see it again either.

Ted Turner

Old age is an island surrounded by death.

Juan Montalvo

'Leave the dead to bury their dead.' There is not a single word of Christ to which the Christian religion has paid less attention.

André Gide

Life is not a dress rehearsal.

Paul Hogan

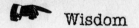

If we do not live now, when do we begin?

J. B. Priestley

Anyone who makes a lot of money quickly must be pretty crooked – honest pushing away at the grindstone never made anyone a bomb.

Marilyn Rice-Davies

It is said that sheep may get lost simply by nibbling away at the grass and never looking up. That can be true for any of us. We can focus so much on what is immediately before us that we fail to see life in larger perspective.

Donald Bitsberger

The living are the dead on holiday.

Maurice Maeterlinck

It is because everything must come to an end that everything is so beautiful.

Charles Ramuz

The first breath is the beginning of death.

Thomas Fuller

Life and Death

The tyrant dies and his rule is over; the martyr dies and his rule begins.

Sôren Kierkegaard

Death is the night of this turbulent day that we call life.

Bernaedin de St Pierre

The thought of suicide is a powerful comfort; it helps one through many a dreadful night.

Friedrich Nietzsche

Only two things are certain in this world – death and ingratitude.

Denis Hamilton

Life is a series of crises separated by brief periods of self-delusion.

Richard Rosen

You are here only for a short visit. Don't hurry, don't worry. And be sure to smell the flowers along the way.

Walter Hagen

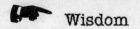

If I had known that death would be this easy, I wouldn't have worried about it.

> Bobby Jones

It is better to live rich than to die rich.

> Samuel Johnson

Let us endeavour so to live that when we come to die even the undertaker will be sorry.

> Mark Twain

I think I will not hang myself today.

> G. K. Chesterton

There are few things easier than to live badly and die well.

> Oscar Wilde

Living is a disease from which sleep gives us relief eight hours a day.

> Nicolas Chamfort

If some died and others did not, death would be a terrible affliction.

> Jean de La Bruyère

Courage is almost a contradiction in terms: it means a strong desire to live taking the form of a readiness to die.

G. K. Chesterton

Many people who spend their time mourning over the brevity of life could make it seem longer if they did a little more work.

Don Marquis

By the time a man is ready to die, he is fit to live.

E. W. Howe

Life is perhaps most widely regarded as a bad dream between two awakenings and every day is a life in miniature.

Eugene O'Neill

Why are we so fond of life that begins with a cry and ends with a groan?

Mary Warwick

More people die in the United States of too much food than of too little food.

J. K. Galbraith

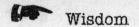

Nobody on his deathbed ever said 'I wish I had spent more time on my job'.

Paul Tsongas

There is nothing terrible in life for the man who realises there is nothing terrible in death.

Epicurus

Death is certain – life is not.

Junior Blair

The meaning of life is that it stops.

Franz Kafka

Death is the cure for all diseases.

Thomas Browne

It's a funny thing about life: if you refuse to accept anything but the very best you will very often get it.

Somerset Maugham

That which does not kill us makes us stronger.

Friedrich Nietzsche

To himself everyone is immortal; he may know
that he is going to die, but he can never know that
he is dead.

Samuel Butler

Man is ready to die for an idea, provided that idea
is not quite clear to him.

Paul Eldridge

The reason so many people never get anywhere in
life is because, when opportunity knocks, they are
out in the backyard looking for four-leaf clovers.

Walter Chrysler

God and Satan

Hell is more bearable than nothingness.

Philip Bailey

The more we understand individual things, the
more we understand God.

Spinoza

I read about an Eskimo hunter who asked the local missionary priest, 'If I did not know about God and sin, would I go to hell?' 'No,' said the priest, 'not if you did not know.' 'Then why,' asked the Eskimo, 'did you tell me?'

Annie Dillard

If you have not known poverty, heart-hunger and misunderstanding, God has overlooked you and you are to be pitied.

Elbert Hubbard

If there were no God there would be no atheists.

G. K. Chesterton

If the devil doesn't exist but man has created him, he has created him in his own image and likeness.

Fyodor Dostoevsky

Modern novelists since and including James Joyce try to represent the whole human mind and soul and yet omit its determining character – that of being God's creature with a defined purpose.

Evelyn Waugh

All that we really know about Hell is that it is a state that exists because God has told us so. We are not bound to believe anyone is in it.

Bruce Marshall

The safest road to Hell is the gradual one – the gentle slope, soft underfoot, without sudden turnings, without milestones, without signposts.

C. S. Lewis

Before God we are all equally wise – equally foolish.

Albert Einstein

I asked a Roman Catholic padre at the front once, what he would do if it was proved to him that there was no God. He replied that it would make no difference to his work at all. He would continue comforting the sick and bereaved, and giving the dying the assurance that there was one who loved them and that their living had not been in vain.

Donald Hankey

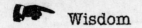

When you first learn to love hell, you will be in heaven.

Thaddeus Golas

Every criminal is an atheist, though he doesn't always know it.

Honoré de Balzac

Parting is all we know of heaven and all we need of hell.

Emily Dickinson

I would rather walk with God in the dark than go alone in the light.

Mary Brainard

It is the quality of our work which will please God and not the quantity.

Mahatma Gandhi

Whom the gods wish to destroy they first call promising.

Cyril Connolly

It is no good casting out devils. They belong to us, we must accept them and be at peace with them.

D. H. Lawrence

The Devil's cleverest ploy is to persuade you that he doesn't exist.

Charles Baudelaire

God Almighty first planted a garden: and indeed it is the purest of pleasures.

Francis Bacon

The devil is a gentleman who never goes where he is not invited.

John A. Lincoln

It is so difficult to forgive God.

Vincent McNabb

Hell is truth seen too late.

Richard Aldington

God asks no man whether he will accept life. That is not the choice. One must take it. The only choice is how.

Henry Ward Beecher

Either God exists or He doesn't. Either I believe in God or I don't. Of the four possibilities, only one is to my disadvantage. To avoid that possibility, I believe in God.

Blaise Pascal

It is certain that whatever seeming calamity happens to you, if you thank and praise God for it, you turn it into a blessing.

William Law

The world is all the richer for having the devil in, so long as we keep our foot upon his neck.

William James

Einstein was a man who could ask immensely simple questions. And what his work showed is that when the answers are simple too, then you can hear God thinking.

Jacob Bronowski

In the absence of any other proof, the thumb alone would convince me of God's existence.

Isaac Newton

God allows the wicked to live to give them time to repent.

Sophie Segur

There is no such thing as an atheist. Everyone believes that he is God.

Alan Ashley-Pitts

Hell is paved with great granite blocks hewn from the hearts of those who said, 'I can do no other'.

Heywood Broun

Part of the fun and mystery of life is that you don't know, but there are hints all over the place. A twinge of conscience is a glimpse of God.

Peter Ustinov

There is wishful thinking in Hell as well as on earth.

Tom Watson

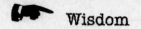

By night an atheist half believes in God.

Edward Young

If you would know what the Lord God thinks of money, you have only to look at those to whom He gives it.

Maurice Baring

God is a comic playing to an audience that's afraid to laugh.

John Ciardi

The Universe is just one of God's thoughts.

Friedrich von Schiller

Many people believe that they are attracted by God, or by Nature, when they are only repelled by man.

W. R. Inge

I do not feel obliged to believe that the same God who endowed us with sense, reason, and intellect intended us to forgo their use.

Galileo Galilei

Ask God's blessing on your work, but don't ask
Him to do it for you.

Flora Robson

He that falls into sin is a man; that grieves at it, is a
saint; that boasts of it, is a devil.

Thomas Fuller

Indigestion is charged by God with enforcing
morality on the stomach.

Victor Hugo

If you can't believe in God, the chances are your
God is too small.

James Phillips

I believe the Bible because I know the author.

Margaret Bottome

Humanity is the sin of God.

Theodore Parker

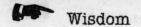

Whom the mad would destroy, they first make gods.

Bernard Levin

The gods conceal from men the happiness of death, that they may endure life.

Lucan

The Devil is easy to identify. He appears when you're tired and makes a very reasonable request which you know you shouldn't grant.

Fiorello La Guardia

Real art is religion, a search for the beauty of God deep in all things.

Emily Carr

If God does not exist, then I am God.

Fyodor Dostoevsky

You never lose the love of God. Guilt is the warning that temporarily you are out of touch.

Jack Dominian

There is not only fun, but there is virtue in a hearty laugh; animals can't laugh, and devils won't.

Josh Billings

Atheism is easy in fair weather.

Ronald Dunn

If you go to Heaven without being naturally qualified for it, you will not enjoy yourself there.

George Bernard Shaw

The Lord has given me both vinegar and honey, but He has given me the vinegar with a teaspoon and the honey with a ladle.

Robert G. Lee

We are all guinea pigs in the laboratory of God. Humanity is just work in progress.

Tennessee Williams

Be careful to preserve your health. It is a trick of the devil, which he employs to deceive good souls, to incite them to do more than they are able in order that they may no longer be able to do anything.

Vincent de Paul

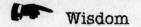

Paradise is made of precisely the same material of which Hell is made. It is only the perception of the order of the materials that differs.

Odysseus Elytis

Among the repulsions of atheism for me has been its drastic uninterestingness as an intellectual position. Where was the ingenuity, the ambiguity, the humanity of saying that the universe just happened to happen and that when we're dead, we are dead?

John Updike

One cannot walk through a mass-production factory and not feel that one is in Hell.

W.H. Auden

God enters by a private door into every individual.

Ralph Waldo Emerson

God will send the bill to you.

James Lowell

A God all mercy is a God unjust.

Edward Young

Can one be a saint if God does not exist?

> Albert Camus

If you don't believe in God, you can suspend it while listening to Bach, and then go back to being an atheist.

> Joan Marsh

O Lord, convert the world and begin with me.

> John Cooper

God is subtle, but He is not malicious.

> Albert Einstein

The hottest places in hell are reserved for those who, in a period of moral crisis, maintain their neutrality.

> Dante

No man can ever enter heaven until he is first convinced he deserves hell.

> John W. Everett

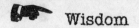

I believe Satan to exist for two reasons; first the Bible says so; and second, I've done business with him.

Dwight L. Moody

When men grow virtuous in their old age they make a sacrifice to God of only the devil's leavings.

Alexander Pope

Sour godliness is the devil's religion.

John Wesley

Let us not be too hasty in judging the Devil. It must be remembered that we have heard only one side of the case, God has written all the books.

Samuel Butler

'My country, right or wrong' is an insult hurled at God.

Jerome K. Jerome

Has this world been so kind to you that you should leave it with regret? There are better things ahead than any we leave behind.

C. S. Lewis

Do not ask God the way to heaven; He will show you the hardest way.

Stanislaw Lec

Of all political ideas, perhaps the most dangerous is the wish to make people perfect and happy. The attempt to realise heaven on earth has always produced a hell.

Karl Popper

When I wrote the Hallelujah Chorus, I thought I did see all Heaven before me, and the Great God Himself.

G.F. Handel

I did not write *Uncle Tom's Cabin*. God wrote it. I merely took his dictation.

Harriet Beecher Stowe

I expect to pass through this world but once; any good thing therefore that I can do, or any kindness that I can show to any fellow creature, let me do it now; let me not defer or neglect it, for I shall not pass this way again.

Stephen Grellet

Although God demands a whole heart, He will accept a broken one if He gets all the pieces.

Mary Irving

Maybe this world is just another planet's hell.

Aldous Huxley

Thousands have gone to heaven who have never read one page of the Bible.

Francis A. Baker

I tremble for my country when I reflect that God is just.

Thomas Jefferson

It takes a long while for a naturally trustful person to reconcile himself to the idea that after all God will not help him.

H. L. Mencken

Lucifer is the patron saint of the visual arts. Colour, form – all these are the work of Lucifer.

Kenneth Anger

Business underlies everything in our natural life, including our spiritual life. Witness the fact that in the Lord's Prayer the first petition is for daily bread. No one can worship God or love his neighbour on an empty stomach.

Woodrow Wilson

God is not dead, but neither is Satan.

C. A. Risley

God gives talent; work transforms it into genius.

Anna Pavlova

You shall have joy or you shall have power, said God; you shall not have both.

Ralph Waldo Emerson

I sometimes think that God, in creating man, somewhat overestimated his ability.

Oscar Wilde

The devil divides the world between atheism and superstition.

George Herbert

I am not afraid that God will destroy the world, but I am afraid that He may abandon it to wander blindly in the sophisticated wasteland of contemporary civilisation.

Carlo Carretto

There is only one thing God cannot do – He cannot please everybody.

Brian Cavanaugh

Man creates God in his own image.

Ernst Haeckel

Light (God's eldest daughter) is a principal beauty in building.

Thomas Fuller

Pain is God's megaphone to rouse a dead world.

C. S. Lewis

God seems to have left the receiver off the hook, and time is running out.

Arthur Koestler

The Lord never spoke of success. He spoke only of faithfulness in love. That is the only success that really counts.

Mother Teresa

No paradise is complete without its snake.

Edith Howie

You'll never get to be a saint if you deny the bit of the devil in you.

Ellis Peters

Every man is his own law court and punishes himself enough.

Patricia Highsmith

To a man with an empty stomach, food is God.

Mahatma Gandhi

I am a great and sublime fool. But then I am God's fool, and all His work must be contemplated with respect.

Mark Twain

Perhaps God is not dead; perhaps God is Himself mad.

R. D. Laing

God designed the stomach to eject what is bad for it, but not the human brain.

Konrad Adenauer

If there is no God, it is up to man to be as moral as he can.

Steve Allen

We know God will forgive us our sins, but what will He think of our virtues?

Peter de Vries

Human Behaviour

The Lord created the universe in seven days but the Lord had the wonderful advantage of being able to work alone.

Kofi Annan

To avoid criticism do nothing, say nothing, be nothing.

Elbert Hubbard

For fast acting relief, try slowing down.

Lily Tomlin

People don't seem to realise how often you have to come in second in order to finish first. I've never met a winner who hadn't learned how to be a loser.

Jack Nicklaus

The most radical revolutionary will become a conservative on the day after the revolution.

Hannah Arendt

Always take on a job that is too big for you.

Harry Fosdick

An eye for an eye and the world would be blind.

Mahatma Gandhi

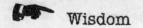

The reward of a thing well done, is to have done it.

Ralph Waldo Emerson

It is very easy to forgive others their mistakes; it takes more grit and gumption to forgive them for having witnessed your own.

Jessamyn West

If you fail, pay your helpers double.

Friedrich Nietzsche

Wealth is like sea-water; the more we drink, the thirstier we become.

Arthur Schopenhauer

Courage is grace under pressure.

Ernest Hemingway

The man who dies rich, dies disgraced.

Andrew Carnegie

I can think of nothing less pleasurable than a life devoted to pleasure.

John D. Rockefeller

If you give a man more than he can do, he will do it. If you give him only what he can do, he will do nothing.

Rudyard Kipling

The need for exercise is a modern superstition invented by people who ate too much, and had nothing to think about.

George Santayana

If you can spend a perfectly useless afternoon in a perfectly useless manner, you have learned to live.

Lin Yutang

We act as though comfort and luxury were the chief requirements of life, when all that we need to make us happy is something to be enthusiastic about.

Charles Kingsley

Work banishes three great evils: boredom, vice and poverty.

Voltaire

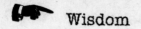

A man who doesn't dream is like a man who doesn't sweat. He stores up a lot of poison.

Truman Capote

Never turn down a small job because you think it's too small – you never know where it can lead.

Julia Morgan

Enthusiasts without capacity are the really dangerous people.

John Maley

If you want a thing done, go. If not, send.

Benjamin Franklin

Any idiot can face a crisis – it's this day-to-day living that wears you out.

Anton Chekhov

It is part of human nature to hate those whom you have injured.

Tacitus

If work were so good, the rich would have hogged it for themselves years ago.

Mark Twain

The greatest mistake you can make in life is to be continually fearing you will make one.

Elbert Hubbard

The highest exercise of charity is charity towards the uncharitable.

J. S. Buckminster

The longer we dwell on our misfortunes, the greater their power to harm us.

Voltaire

Every man cheats in his own way and he is only honest who is not discovered.

Susannah Centlivre

He who has never learned to obey cannot be a good commander.

Aristotle

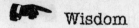

When a dog runs at you, whistle at him.

> Henry D. Thoreau

The finest poems of the world have been
expedients to get bread.

> Ralph Waldo Emerson

Charity deals with symptoms instead of causes.

> George Bernard Shaw

Whenever a man seeks your advice he generally
seeks your praise.

> Lord Chesterfield

You cannot build a reputation on what you're
going to do.

> Henry Ford

There is no end to what you can accomplish if
you don't care who gets the credit.

> Florence Luscomb

A beggar hates his benefactor as much as he hates
himself for begging.

> Oscar Wilde

I have no complex about wealth. I have worked hard for my money producing things people need. I believe that the able industrial leader who creates wealth and employment is more worthy of historical notice than politicians or soldiers.

J. Paul Getty

This is the final test of a gentleman: his respect for those who can be of no possible service to him.

William Phelps

You never forget people who were kind to you when you were young.

Mark Birley

Decorum is just the delicacy of the indelicate.

Walter Raleigh

Don't tell me how hard you work. Tell me how much you get done.

James Ling

People's minds are changed through observation and not through argument.

Will Rogers

Never let your inferiors do you a favour. It will be extremely costly.

H. L. Mencken

Opportunity is missed by most people because it is dressed in overalls and looks like work.

Thomas Edison

Why inflict pain on oneself, when so many others are ready to save us the trouble?

George Pacaud

Tell them the truth; first because it is the right thing to do and second they'll find out anyway.

Paul Galvin

We dig our graves each day with our teeth.

Samuel Smiles

Many a man is saved from being a thief by finding everything locked up.

E.W. Howe

I don't believe in just ordering people to do things. You have to sort of grab an oar and row with them.

Harold Geneen

Examining one's entrails while fighting a battle is a recipe for certain defeat.

Denis Healey

Delay is the deadliest form of denial.

C. Northcote Parkinson

When once a people have tasted the luxury of not paying their debts, it is impossible to bring them back to the black broth of honesty.

Sydney Smyth

Talk low, talk slow and don't say too much.

John Wayne

'I can forgive but I cannot forget' is another way of saying 'I cannot forgive'.

Henry Ward Beecher

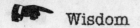

Nothing is often a good thing to do and always a good thing to say.

Will Durant

The smallest good deed is better than the grandest good invention.

Duguet

Man is a wanting animal — as soon as one of his needs is satisfied, another appears in its place. This process is unending. It continues from birth to death.

Douglas McGregor

The art of life lies in a constant readjustment to our surroundings.

Okakura Kakuzo

I praise loudly, I blame softly.

Catherine the Great

Living at risk is jumping off the cliff and building your wings on the way down.

Ray Bradbury

Look over your shoulder now and again to be sure someone is following you.

Henry Gilmer

The bird of paradise alights only upon the hand that does not grasp.

John Berry

Fair and softly goes far.

Miguel de Cervantes

You don't get any marks for trying; you must actually succeed. I am not interested in any sophisticated reasons for failure.

Allen Sheppard

The way to make money is to buy when blood is running in the streets.

John D. Rockefeller Jr

A happy man may be a successful bishop, dog-catcher, movie actor or sausage-monger, but no happy man ever produced a first-rate piece of painting, sculpture, music or literature.

J. G. Nathan

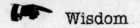

I am surprised nothing has been made of the fact that when astronaut Neil Armstrong landed on the moon, he carried no arms.

Arthur Goldberg

This war, like the next war, is a war to end wars.

David Lloyd George

Beware of those who laugh at everything or nothing.

Arnold Glasow

Always remember others may hate you but those who hate you don't win unless you hate them. And then you destroy yourself.

Richard Nixon

The key to everything is patience. You get the chicken by hatching the egg, not by smashing it.

Arnold Glasow

Don't find a fault – find a remedy.

Henry Ford

The truest health is to be able to get on without it.

Robert Louis Stevenson

The darkest hour of any man's life is when he sits down to plan how to get money without earning it.

Horace Greeley

The stupid neither forgive nor forget; the naïve forgive and forget; the wise forgive but do not forget.

Thomas Szasz

Next to knowing when to seize an opportunity, the most important thing in life is to know when to forgo an advantage.

Benjamin Disraeli

Work is something you can always count on, a trusted, lifelong friend who never deserts you.

Margaret Bourke-White

Words of comfort skilfully administered are the oldest therapy known to man.

George Bernard Shaw

Men hate those to whom they have to lie.

Victor Hugo

A bone to the dog is not charity. Charity is the bone shared with the dog, when you are just as hungry as the dog.

Jack London

Swing hard, in case they throw the ball where you're swinging.

Duke Snider

If your ship doesn't come in, swim out to it.

Jonathon Winters

Better break your word than do worse in keeping it.

Thomas Fuller

Whatever you do will be insignificant, but it is very important that you do it.

Mahatma Gandhi

The best cure for hypochondria is to forget about your body and get interested in someone else's.

Ace Goodman

The roulette table pays nobody except him who keeps it. Nevertheless, a passion for gaming is common, though a passion for keeping roulette wheels is unknown.

George Bernard Shaw

Never esteem anything as of advantage to you that will make you break your word or lose your self-respect.

Marcus Antoninus

A conquered foe should be watched.

E. W. Howe

Little minds are wounded by the smallest things.

La Rochefoucauld

One never notices what has been done; one can see only what remains to be done.

Marie Curie

All hatred is self-hatred.

Dominic Cleary

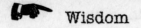

Hatred is self-punishment.

Hosea Ballou

The liar's punishment is not in the least that he is not believed, but that he cannot believe anyone else.

George Bernard Shaw

Where large sums of money are concerned, it is advisable to trust nobody.

Agatha Christie

When you join the Parachute Regiment they send you on training and initiation exercises. One of the tasks is to accept and care for a pet white rabbit. The young squaddie has to feed, brush, stroke and comfort his rabbit for a week and become attached to it. Then he has to shoot it.

Matthew Parris

Good resolutions are simply cheques that men draw on a bank where they have no account.

Oscar Wilde

Give, expecting nothing thereof.

Thomas Aquinas

If you see a tennis player who looks as if he is working hard, that means he isn't very good.

Helen Wills Moody

The best manner of avenging ourselves is by not resembling him who has injured us.

Jane Porter

Do not do what you would undo if caught.

Leah Arendt

Craziness is doing the same thing and expecting a different result.

Tom De Marco

People will never know how long it takes you to do something. They will only know how well it is done.

Nancy Hanks

If you have built castles in the air, your work need not be lost – that is where they should be. Now put foundations under them.

Henry D. Thoreau

No example is so dangerous as that of violence employed by well-meaning people for beneficial objects.

Alexis de Tocqueville

All men practise the actor's art.

Petronius

If you cannot feed a million people, then feed just one.

Mother Teresa

It is a mistake to look too far ahead. Only one link in the chain of destiny can be handled at a time.

Winston Churchill

No lunatic with the gift of oratory is harmless.

Dan Binchy

There is no such thing as a great talent without great willpower.

Honoré de Balzac

No path of flowers leads to glory.

La Fontaine

Start by doing what is necessary, then what's possible and suddenly you're doing the impossible.

> St Francis of Assisi

The commonest instruments of suicide are a knife and fork.

> Martin Fischer

Shallow men believe in luck. Strong men believe in cause and effect.

> Ralph Waldo Emerson

You can give without loving, but you cannot love without giving.

> Amy Carmichael

There are many things that we would throw away, if we were not afraid that others might pick them up.

> Oscar Wilde

When I was young I observed that nine out of ten things I did were failures, so I did ten times more work.

> George Bernard Shaw

Amateurs hope. Professionals work.

Garson Kanin

Doing easily what others find difficult is talent;
doing what is impossible for talent is genius.

Henri Amiel

A small daily task, if it be really daily, will beat the
labours of a spasmodic Hercules.

Anthony Trollope

Guts is grace under pressure.

Ernest Hemingway

How shall the diver obtain pearls if he wrestles not
with the terrors of the deep?

Ibn Yamin

Always be a little kinder than necessary.

J. M. Barrie

Endure, and preserve yourself for better things.

Virgil

Laughter has always seemed to me to be the most civilised music in the universe.

Peter Ustinov

A prosperous fool is a grievous burden.

Aeschylus

Temperate temperance is best; intemperate temperance injures the cause of temperance.

Mark Twain

Few things are impossible to diligence and skill. Great works are performed, not by strength, but by perseverance.

Samuel Johnson

In a longish life as a professional writer, I have heard a thousand masterpieces talked out over bars, restaurant tables and love seats. I have never seen one of them in print. Books must be written, not talked.

Morris West

Every man who ever created anything was a gambler.

Kerry Packer

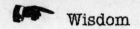

Half our life is spent trying to find something to do with the time we have rushed through life trying to save.

Will Rogers

He can keep silence well. That man's silence is wonderful to listen to.

Thomas Hardy

When it comes to getting things done, we need fewer architects and more bricklayers.

Colleen Barrett

Persistence is the hard work that you do after you are tired of doing the hard work you already did.

Newt Gingrich

A person needs a little madness, or else they never dare cut the rope and be free.

Nikos Kazantzakis

If you suffer and forgive those who made you suffer, you are the stronger of the two.

Derek Ivany

Apostles of Freedom are ever idolised when dead, but crucified when alive.

James Connolly

What a lot we lost when we stopped writing letters. You cannot reread a phone call.

Liz Carpenter

We continue to overlook the fact that work has become a leisure activity.

Mark Abrams

Beware of the barrenness of a busy life.

Socrates

It takes a strong man to be mean. A mean man is one that has the courage not to be generous.

Finley Peter Dunne

Learn how to fail intelligently, for failing is one of the greatest arts in the world.

Charles Kettering

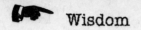

The worst-tempered people I have ever met were those who knew that they were in the wrong.

Wilson Mizner

Look twice before you leap.

Charlotte Brontë

It never occurs to fools that merit and fortune are closely united.

J. W. von Goethe

He who is slowest in making a promise is most faithful in its performance.

Jean-Jacques Rousseau

There is nothing in the world stronger than gentleness.

Han Suyin

The secret of happiness is to admire without desiring.

F.H. Bradley

Impatient people always arrive too late.

Jean Dutourd

I believe you are your work. Don't trade the stuff of your life, time, for nothing more than dollars. That's a rotten bargain.

Rita Mae Brown

The best aim in business is to make money out of satisfying customers.

John Egan

Great eaters and great sleepers are not capable of doing anything great.

Henri IV

Why go miles and miles to see the dubious stigmata on someone's hands, yet not move a step to contemplate the sore-covered hands of the poor?

Carlo Carretto

The secret of success is to do the common things uncommonly well.

John D. Rockefeller Jr.

Many attempts to communicate are nullified by saying too much.

Robert Greenleaf

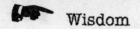

A stiff apology is a second insult.

G. K. Chesterton

Tomorrow God isn't going to ask what did you dream, what did you think, what did you plan, what did you preach? He's going to ask, What did you do?

Michel Quoist

We are dismayed when we find that even disaster cannot cure us of our faults.

Vauvenargues

The principal act of courage is to endure and withstand dangers doggedly rather than to attack them.

Thomas Aquinas

Good swimmers are oftenest drowned.

Thomas Fuller

Whenever I hear anyone arguing for slavery, I feel a strong impulse to see it tried on him personally.

Abraham Lincoln

Action is the last refuge of those who cannot dream.

Oscar Wilde

Every time a man laughs heartily, he takes a kink out of the chain that binds him to life and thus lengthens it.

Josh Billings

If you have to do it every day, for God's sake learn to do it well.

Mignon McLaughlin

The cruellest lies are often told in silence.

Robert Louis Stevenson

Tolerance is another word for indifference.

Somerset Maugham

The greatest analgesic, soporific, stimulant, tranquiliser, narcotic, and to some extent even antibiotic – in short the closest thing to a genuine panacea known to medical science is work.

Thomas Szasz

It is really not so repulsive to see the poor asking for money. And advertisement is the rich asking for more money.

G.K. Chesterton

While seeking revenge, dig two graves – one for yourself.

Doug Horton

Remember that in giving any reason at all for refusing, you lay some foundation for a future request.

Arthur Helps

No man has a good enough memory to be a successful liar.

Abraham Lincoln

It wasn't raining when Noah built the ark.

Howard Ruff

When someone holds nothing but trumps, it is impossible to play cards.

Christian Hebbel

A man who has to be convinced before he acts is not a man of action. You must act as you breathe.

> Georges Clemenceau

Scoundrels are always sociable.

> Arthur Schopenhauer

Go uphill as fast as you please; but go downhill slowly.

> John Billings

Never try to pacify someone at the height of their rage.

> Esther Selsdon

The car, the furniture, the wife, the children – everything has to be disposable. Because you see the main thing today is shopping.

> Arthur Miller

There is a right way and a wrong way to do everything and the wrong way is to keep trying to make everybody else do it the right way.

> Harry Morgan

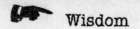

A pessimist is one who makes difficulties of his opportunities; an optimist is one who makes opportunities of his difficulties.

Reginald Mansell

It is better to fail in originality than to succeed in imitation.

Herman Melville

If you want to succeed, double your failure rate.

Tom Watson

Habit is overcome by habit.

Thomas à Kempis

A life of pleasure is the most unpleasing life in the world.

Oliver Goldsmith

Take sides. Neutrality helps the oppressor, never the victim. Silence encourages the tormentor, never the tormentee.

Elie Wiesel

Sooner or later everyone sits down to a banquet of consequences.

Frank Gannon

If we had no winter, the spring would not be so pleasant; if we did not sometimes taste of adversity, prosperity would not be so welcome.

Anne Bradstreet

Resolved: never to do anything which I should be afraid to do if it were the last hour of my life.

Jonathan Edwards

If you had only six months to live, what would you do, and if you're not doing that now, why not?

Stephen Thomas

No man is an island, entire of itself; every man is a piece of the Continent, a part of the main. Any man's death diminishes me, because I am involved in mankind; therefore never send to know for whom the bell tolls, it tolls for thee.

John Donne

To enjoy freedom we have to control ourselves.

Virginia Woolf

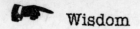

Tough times don't last, tough people do.

Robert Schuller

No people do so much harm as those who go about doing good.

Mandell Creighton

A large part of altruism, even when it is perfectly honest, is grounded upon the fact that it is uncomfortable to have unhappy people about one.

H. L. Mencken

Nothing arouses ambition so much in the heart as the trumpet clang of another's fame.

Baltasar Gracian

Liberty too can corrupt, and absolute liberty can corrupt absolutely.

Gertrude Himmelfarls

How wise are thy commandments, Lord. Each of them applies to somebody I know.

Sam Levenson

If two men on the same job agree all the time, then one is useless. If they disagree all the time, then both are useless.

Darryl Zanuck

Charity that is always beginning at home stays there.

Austin O'Malley

The man who first abused his fellows with swear-words, instead of bashing their brains out with a club, should be counted among those who laid the foundations of civilisation.

John Cohen

I cannot give you the formula for success, but I can give you the formula for failure. Try to please everybody.

Herbert B. Swope

True generosity consists precisely in fighting to destroy the causes which nourish false charity.

Paulo Freire

Leave the beaten track occasionally and dive into the woods. You will be certain to find something you have never seen before.

Alexander Graham Bell

A long dispute means that both parties are wrong.

Bob Phillips

The worst thing I ever said to an umpire was 'are you sure?'

Rod Laver

Anyone who has lived his life to the fullest extent has a scandal buried somewhere. And anybody who doesn't, I have no interest in meeting. You show me somebody who has led a perfect life and I'll show you a dullard.

Rob Lowe

He who praises everybody, praises nobody.

Samuel Johnson

He that has a secret should not only hide it, but hide that he has it to hide.

Thomas Carlyle

The world is for the most part, a collective madhouse, and practically everyone, however 'normal' his facade, is faking sanity.

John Astin

You can get through life with bad manners – but it's easier with good manners.

Lillian Gish

Kindness is a language which the deaf can hear and the blind can read.

Mark Twain

Blessed is the person who is too busy to worry in the daytime, and too sleepy to worry at night.

Leo Ackman

One of the deadliest things on earth is a cheerful person with no sense of humour.

G. K. Chesterton

Good breeding consists in concealing how much we think of ourselves and how little we think of the other person.

Mark Twain

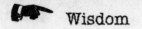

To practise what we preach is rightly expected, but to preach what we practise would be to invite suspicion.

Arnold Haller

You can sign a thousand autographs, but walk away with two or three left stranded and you are branded as too big and rich to bother with the common man.

Fred Couples

No one gossips about other people's secret virtues.

Bertrand Russell

Where is human nature so weak as in a bookstore?

Henry Ward Beecher

Three may keep a secret if two of them are dead.

Benjamin Franklin

Never cut what you can untie.

Joseph Joubert

Millionaires seldom laugh.

Andrew Carnegie

Nothing is illegal if a hundred businessmen decide to do it.

Andrew Young

Every American crusade winds up as a racket.

John P. Roche

The absurd person is the one who never changes.

Auguste Barthélémy

We must interpret a bad temper as a sign of inferiority.

Alfred Adler

All man's troubles come from not knowing how to sit still in one room.

Blaise Pascal

Advertising is legalised lying.

H. G. Wells

Since when do you have to agree with people to defend them from injustice?

Lillian Hellman

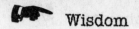

Wild animals never kill for sport. Man is the only one to whom the torture and death of his fellow creatures is amusing in itself.

James A. Froude

What one has to do usually can be done.

Eleanor Roosevelt

Remember, no one can make you feel inferior without your consent.

Eleanor Roosevelt

The mass of men lead lives of quiet desperation.

Henry D. Thoreau

If you can play as if it means nothing when it means everything, then you are hard to beat.

Steve Davis

Take a rest; a field that has rested gives a beautiful crop.

Ovid

Eighty per cent of success is just showing up.

Woody Allen

The test of a vocation is the love of the drudgery it involves.

Logan Pearsall Smith

Hypocrisy is a sort of homage that vice pays virtue.

Thomas Fuller

Laws are spider webs through which the big flies pass and the little ones get caught.

Honoré de Balzac

Facing the press is more difficult than bathing a leper.

Mother Teresa

No innocent man buys a gun and no happy man writes his memoirs.

Raymond Payne

Gluttony is an emotional escape, a sign something is eating us.

Peter de Vries

Perhaps the straight and narrow path would be wider if more people used it.

Kay Ingram

The reasonable man adapts himself to the world, but the unreasonable man tries to adapt the world to him. Therefore, all progress depends on the unreasonable man.

Samuel Butler

Nobody ever had to call a penalty for rules violation on me – I'd call it on myself.

Ben Hogan

Put all your eggs in one basket – and watch that basket.

Mark Twain

If all mankind were suddenly to practise honesty, many thousands of people would be sure to starve.

G. C. Lichtenberg

People forget how fast you did a job – but they remember how well you did it.

Howard Newton

The only argument against an east wind is to put on your overcoat.

James Lowell

He who is afraid of every nettle should not piss in the grass.

Thomas Fuller

Beggars should be abolished – it is irritating to give to them and it is irritating not to.

Friedrich Nietzsche

White lies by frequent use become black ones.

Douglas Jerrold

Everyone is a moon and has a dark side which he never shows to anybody.

Mark Twain

If a man can remember what he worried about last week, he has a very good memory.

Woody Allen

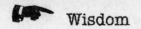

A person reveals his character by nothing so
clearly as the joke he resents.

G. C. Lichtenberg

Never confuse a single mistake with a final
mistake.

F. Scott Fitzgerald

Don't play for safety – it's the most dangerous
thing in the world.

Hugh Walpole

Laziness travels so slowly that poverty soon
overtakes him.

Benjamin Franklin

Don't be afraid to take a big step if one is
indicated; you can't cross a chasm in two small
jumps.

David Lloyd George

If you are going to be cheap, do not be cheap with
the seed.

Jack Exum

The winds and the waves are always on the side of the ablest navigators.

Edward Gibbon

Blessed are those who can give without remembering, and take without forgetting.

Elizabeth Bibesco

I can pardon everyone's mistakes but my own.

Marcus Cato

The best way to get a bad law repealed is to enforce it strictly.

Abraham Linçoln

It is the most guilty bastard in the crowd who casts the first stone.

William McIlvanney

I have found men more kind than I expected, and less just.

Samuel Johnson

Every obnoxious act is a cry for help.

Zig Ziglar

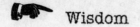

If you hoe where there are no weeds then there will be no weeds.

Michael Z. Lewin

Although there exist many thousand subjects for elegant conversation, there are persons who cannot meet a cripple without talking about feet.

Ernest Bramah

A hole in the ice is dangerous only to those who go skating.

Rex Stout

The most difficult instrument to play in the orchestra is second fiddle. I can get plenty of first violinists, but to find someone who can play second fiddle with enthusiasm – that's the problem. Yet, if there is no one to play second fiddle, there is no harmony.

Leonard Bernstein

Most people sell their souls and live with a good conscience on the proceeds.

Logan Pearsall Smith

Never stand begging for what you have the power to earn.

Miguel de Cervantes

The best preparation for tomorrow is to do today's work superbly well.

William Osler

Don't be afraid to give your best to what are seemingly small jobs. Every time you conquer one it makes you that much stronger. If you do the little jobs well, the big ones will tend to take care of themselves.

Dale Carnegie

It is often pleasant to stone a martyr, no matter how much we admire him.

John Barth

It is by sitting down to write every morning that one becomes a writer. Those who do not do this remain amateurs.

Gerald Brenan

People often feed the hungry so that nothing may disturb their own enjoyment of a good meal.

Somerset Maugham

If you cannot win, make the fellow in front of you break the record.

Desmond Cleary

I found that the men and women who got to the top were those who did the jobs they had in hand, with everything they had of energy and enthusiasm and hard work.

Harry S. Truman

It is not wise to violate the rules until you know how to observe them.

T. S. Eliot

Don't ever take a fence down until you know the reason why it was put up.

G. K. Chesterton

Addictions and Obsessions

The art of cookery is the art of poisoning mankind, by rendering the appetite still importunate, when the wants of nature are supplied.

Francois Fénelon

I do not drink because I was born intoxicated.

George Russell

A man who has not passed through the inferno of his passions has never overcome them.

Carl Jung

The more necessary it becomes to stop drinking, the more impossible it becomes to stop.

Jeffrey Bernard

No man has ever pulled himself out of his troubles with troubles.

J. Tudor Rees

Drunkenness is nothing but voluntary madness.

Seneca

Of all tyrannies which have been usurped power
over humanity, few have been able to enslave the
mind and the body as imperiously as drug
addiction.

Freda Adler

Drunkenness is temporary suicide: the happiness it
brings is merely negative, a momentary cessation
of unhappiness.

Bertrand Russell

Do not bite at the bait of pleasure till you know
there is no hook.

Thomas Jefferson

Time spent in a casino is time given to death, a
foretaste to the hour when one's flesh will be
diverted to the purposes of the worm and not the
will.

Rebecca West

Lust is the craving for salt of a man who is dying
of thirst.

Friedrich Buechner

You never know what is enough, until you know what is more than enough.

William Blake

Fame, like a drunkard, consumes the house of the soul.

Malcolm Lowry

Pornography is a successful attempt to sell sex for more than it's worth.

Quentin Crisp

There is more refreshment and stimulation in a nap, even of the briefest, than in all the alcohol ever distilled.

E.V. Lucas

The truest gourmet, like the true artist, is one of the unhappiest creatures existent. His trouble comes from so seldom finding what he constantly seeks – perfection.

Ludwig Beethoven

Whipping and abuse are like laudanum; you have to double the dose as the sensibilities decline.

Harriet Beecher Stowe

What is dangerous about tranquillisers is that whatever peace of mind they bring is a packaged peace of mind. Where you buy a pill and buy peace of mind with it, you get conditioned to cheap solutions instead of deep ones.

Max Lerner

Victims of drunk drivers have no place to turn. Judges drink and drive, juries drink and drive, D.A.'s drink and drive. They're going to have sympathy for the drunk driver. They don't have sympathy for the rapist, the murderer, the mugger.

Candy Lightner

If something bad happens, you drink in order to forget; if something good happens you drink in order to celebrate; and if nothing happens, you drink in order to make something happen.

Charles Bukowski

Pot is like a gang of Mexican bandits in your brain. They wait for thoughts to come down the road, then tie them up and thrash them.

Kevin Rooney

Succeed we must, at all cost – even if it means being a dead millionaire at fifty.

Louis Kronenberger

No man ever repented that he arose from the table sober, healthful and with his wits about him.

Jeremy Taylor

Is it the fault of wine if a fool drinks it and goes stumbling into darkness?

Avicenna

Profanity is a brutal vice. He who indulges in it is no gentleman.

Edwin Chapin

For premature adventure one pays an atrocious price. Every boy I know who drank at eighteen or nineteen is now safe in his grave.

F. Scott Fitzgerald

Common people do not pray; they only beg.

George Bernard Shaw

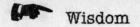

To suppose that we could be rich and not behave as the rich behave is like supposing that we could drink all day and keep absolutely sober.

Logan Pearsall Smith

Instant gratification is soon not enough.

Carrie Fisher

I am a child of an alcoholic. I know about promises.

Sandra Scoppettone

If alcohol were a communicable disease, a national emergency would be declared.

William Menninger

As bees their sting, so the promiscuous leave behind them in each encounter something of themselves by which they are made to suffer.

Cyril Connolly

Drowning your sorrows only irrigates them.

Ken Alstad

Habit is a cable; we weave a thread of it every day, and at last we cannot break it.

Horace Mann

Addiction is an increasing desire for an act which gives less and less satisfaction.

Aldous Huxley

The cat, having sat upon a hot stove lid, will not sit upon a hot stove lid again. Nor upon a cold stove lid.

Mark Twain

Abstinence is as easy to me as temperance would be difficult.

Samuel Johnson

You don't gamble to win. You gamble so you can gamble the next day.

Bert Ambrose

A drunk is a person who could stop drinking if only he would. An alcoholic is a person who would stop drinking if only he could.

Tom Shipp

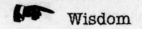

After a certain point, money is meaningless. It
ceases to be the goal. The game is what counts.

Aristotle Onassis

He who wishes to be rich in a day will be hanged
in a day.

Leonardo da Vinci

The sight of a drunkard is a better sermon against
that vice than the best that was ever preached on
that subject.

Horatio Saville

Money brings some happiness but after a certain
point it just brings more money.

Neil Simon

The wish to hurt, the momentary intoxication
with pain, is the loophole through which the
pervert climbs into the minds of ordinary men.

Jacob Bronowski

All isms end in fascism.

Gilbert Adair

I have enough work to make me rich beyond my wildest dreams. But I've met many millionaires and they've all been miserable.

Tom Keating

A credit card is an anaesthetic which simply delays the pain.

Helen Mason

When you have found out the prevailing passion of any man, remember never to trust him as far as that passion is concerned.

Lord Chesterfield

The worst drug of today is not smack or pot — it's refined sugar.

George Hamilton

No man is smart enough to be funny when he is drunk.

E.W. Howe

You can have too much champagne to drink, but you can never have enough.

Elmer Rice

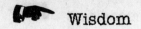

I like whiskey, I always have, and that's why I never drink it.

Robert E. Lee

I am more afraid of alcohol than of all the bullets of the enemy.

Stonewall Jackson

Fanaticism is just one step away from barbarism.

Denis Diderot

As a cure for worrying, work is better than whiskey.

Thomas Edison

Youth and Age

Live as long as you may, the first twenty years are the longest half of your life.

Robert Southey

The hardest job kids face today is learning good manners without seeing any.

Fred Astaire

I do not ask to be young again; all I want is to go on getting older.

Konrad Adenauer

Childhood sometimes does pay a second visit to man; youth never.

Anna Jameson

Growing old is like being increasingly penalised for a crime you haven't committed.

Anthony Powell

Beware of what you wish for in youth, for in middle age you will surely achieve it.

J.W. von Goethe

Babylon in all its desolation is a sight not so awful as that of the human mind in ruins.

Scrope Berdmore Davies

Old age puts more wrinkles in our minds than on our faces.

Michel de Montaigne

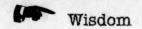

The dead might as well try to speak to the living
as the old to the young.

Willa Cather

Age is a high price to pay for maturity.

Tom Stoppard

Don't complain about growing old – many people
are denied that privilege.

Earl Warren

Old and young, we are all on our last cruise.

Robert Louis Stevenson

The young stagger along the primrose path of
pleasure, mistakenly believing that it leads to
happiness until their nerves are frayed to bits.

Quentin Crisp

One starts to get young at the age of sixty and
then it's too late.

Pablo Picasso

Older men declare war. But it is youth that must fight and die.

> Herbert Hoover

The first forty years of life give us the text; the last thirty supply the commentary.

> Arthur Schopenhauer

There is always one moment in childhood when the door opens and lets the future in.

> Graham Greene

The first sign of maturity is the discovery that the volume knob also turns to the left.

> 'Smile' Zingers

In a dream you are never eighty.

> Anne Sexton

Childhood decides.

> Jean-Paul Sartre

Time is a dressmaker specialising in alterations.

> Faith Baldwin

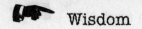

Children have never been very good at listening to their elders, but they have never failed to imitate them.

James Baldwin

In my day, we didn't have self-esteem, we had self-respect, and no more of it than we had earned.

Jane Haddam

We have not passed that subtle line between childhood and adulthood until we move from the passive voice to the active voice – that is until we have stopped saying 'It got lost', and say, 'I lost it'.

Sydney Harris

Young men think old men are fools; but old men know young men are fools.

George Chapman

Alas! It is not the child, but the boy that generally survives in the man.

Arthur Helps

When your son is six, make him obey. When your son is sixteen, make him a friend.

Brian Aldiss

You have to do your own growing no matter how tall your grandfather was.

Abraham Lincoln

Give me the children until they are seven and anyone may have them afterwards.

Francis Xavier

Growing old is no more than a bad habit which a busy man has no time to form.

André Maurois

When childhood dies, its corpses are called adults and they enter society, one of the politer names of hell. That is why we dread children, even if we love them, they show us the state of our decay.

Brian Aldiss

The tragedy of old age is not that one is old, but that one is young.

Oscar Wilde

Old age is the out-patients' department of purgatory.

David Cecil

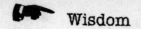

What attracts young men is the sight of the zeal
that surrounds a cause.

Friedrich Nietzsche

No one grows old by living – only by losing
interest in living.

Marie Ray

The young do not know enough to be prudent;
and, therefore, they attempt the impossible – and
achieve it, generation after generation.

Pearl S. Buck

No wise man ever wished to be younger.

Jonathan Swift

One of the most obvious facts about grown ups to
a child is that they have forgotten what it is like to
be a child.

Randall Jarrell

Old age is life's unsafe harbour.

Elliot Priest

What is called youth is not youth; it is rather something like premature old age.

> Henry Miller

There is a tendency to keep slightly away from old bodies. I think the old need touching. They have reached a stage in life when they need kissing, hugging. And nobody touches them except the doctor.

> Ron Blythe

Men and Women

The success of the marriage comes after the failure of the honeymoon.

> G. K. Chesterton

I do not trust men who run after every woman — this is not the way to win revolutions. Revolution needs concentration, a heightening of forces. The wild excesses of sexual life are reactionary symptoms.

> V. I. Lenin

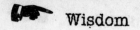

A divorce is like an amputation; you survive, but there's less of you.

Margaret Atwood

Marriage is three parts love and seven parts forgiveness.

Langdon Mitchell

Why are women so much more interesting to men than men are to women?

Virginia Woolf

If civilisation had been left in female hands, we would still be living in grass huts.

Camille Paglia

Marriage is like a cage: one sees the birds outside desperate to get in, and those inside equally desperate to get out.

Michel de Montaigne

Making love without love is like trying to make a soufflé without egg whites.

Simone Beck

Ah, women. They make the highs higher and the lows more frequent.

Friedrich Nietzsche

The older woman flirts with a self-controlled awareness which can make her assaults much more deadly than the blind rushes of the young.

Iris Murdoch

Seduction is a circulating library in which we seldom ask for the same volume.

Nathaniel Willis

I have always found it best to appear to yield. Assume a seeming conformity to your husband's will and you will more easily get the reins into your hands.

Catherine de Medici

The quarrels of lovers are like summer showers that leave the country more verdant and beautiful.

Marie Nickin

Love built on beauty soon as beauty dies.

John Donne

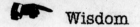

The fall, like the serpent, was mythical: the apple was sound and Eve hysterical.

Eva Lathbury

Women lie about their age; men lie about their income.

William Feather

Man is not the enemy of woman, but the fellow victim.

Betty Friedan

The finest people marry the two sexes in their own person.

Ralph Waldo Emerson

There are but two objects in marriage, love or money. If you marry for love, you will certainly have some very happy days and probably many very uneasy ones; if you marry for money, you will have no happy days and probably no uneasy ones.

Lord Chesterfield

Marriage is a job – happiness or unhappiness has nothing to do with it.

Kathleen Norris

Getting married is easy. Staying married is more difficult. Staying happily married for a lifetime should rank among the finest arts.

Roberta Flack

The sum which two married people owe to one another defies calculation. It is an infinite debt, which can be discharged only through all eternity.

J.W. von Goethe

I thought when love for you died, I should die. It's dead. Alone, mostly strangely, I live on.

Rupert Brooke

It is the personality of the mistress of the house that the home expresses. Men are forever guests in our own homes, no matter how much happiness they may find there.

Elsie De Wolfe

The longest absence is less perilous to love than the terrible trials of incessant proximity.

Ouida

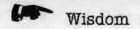

I haven't yet been able to find a happy adulterer.

Tamasin Day-Lewis

A marriage without conflicts is almost as inconceivable as a nation without crises.

André Maurois

May I be looking at you when my last hour has come, and as I die may I hold you with my weakening hand.

Tibullus

The married state is the most complete image of heaven and hell we are capable of receiving in this life.

Richard Steele

There is no word equivalent to 'cuckold' for women.

Joseph Epstein

What is most beautiful in virile men is something feminine; what is most beautiful in feminine women is something masculine.

Susan Sontag

When you get the personality, you don't need the nudity.

Mae West

Man and woman are two locked caskets, of which each contains the key to the other.

Isak Dinesen

There is not one female comedian who was beautiful as a little girl.

Joan Rivers

Love is what you've been through with somebody.

James Thurber

You don't marry one person; you marry three: the person you think they are, the person they are, and the person they are going to become as the result of being married to you.

Richard Needham

In every marriage more than a week old, there are grounds for divorce. The trick is to find, and continue to find, grounds for marriage.

Robert Anderson

Next to the wound, what women make best is the bandage.

Barbey D'Aurevilly

Strength and gentleness. Men have cultivated the one and women the other. Do thou cultivate both.

John Penyfield

All that a husband or wife really wants is to be pitied a little, praised a little, appreciated a little.

Oliver Goldsmith

Men can be analysed, women merely adored.

Oscar Wilde

One man, two loves. No good ever comes of that.

Euripides

Women keep a special corner of their hearts for sins they have never committed.

Cornelia Otis Skinner

A woman's heart always has a burned mark.

Louise Labé

If the man and woman walk off into the sunset
hand in hand in the last reel, it adds $10 million to
the box office.

George Lucas

A girl who thinks that a man will treat her better
after marriage than before is a fool.

William C. Hall

Nearly all marriages, even happy ones, are mistakes
in the sense that almost certainly both partners
might have found more suitable mates. But the real
soul-mate is the one you are actually married to.

J. R. R. Tolkien

It is delightful to be a woman; but every man
thanks the Lord devoutly that he isn't one.

Olive Schreiner

He knows little who will tell his wife all he
knows.

Thomas Fuller

An undutiful daughter will prove an
unmanageable wife.

Benjamin Franklin

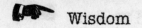

Every marriage is a battle between two families struggling to reproduce themselves.

Carl Whitaker

Because of its secret nature, you should not talk or write about sex. You can love talk with the person you're in love with – that's a different matter. But any talk of sex with others is anti-human.

Robert Graves

There is nothing safe about sex. There never will be.

Norman Mailer

Women are natural guerillas. Scheming, we nestle into the enemy's bed, avoiding open warfare, watching the options, playing the odds.

Sally Kempton

After marriage, a woman's sight becomes so keen that she can see right through her husband without looking at him, and a man's so dull that he can look right through his wife without seeing her.

Helen Rowland

In the arithmetic of love, one plus one equals everything, and two minus one equals nothing.

Mignon McLaughlin

The desire engendered in the male glands is a hundred times more difficult to control than the desire bred in the female glands. All girls who limit their actions to arousing desire and then defending their virtue should be horsewhipped.

Marlene Dietrich

Promiscuity in women is illness, a leakage of identity. The promiscuous woman is self-contaminated and incapable of clear ideas. She has ruptured the ritual integrity of her body.

Camille Paglia

The pretentiously named ensuite bathroom is a major factor in divorce. Privacy is paramount in marriage.

Steve Updike

The compulsion to find a lover and a husband in a single person has doomed more women to misery than any other illusion.

Carolyn Heilbrun

My advice to those who think they have to take their clothes off to be a star is, once you're boned, what's left to create the illusion? Let 'em wonder. I never believed in givin' them too much of me.

Mae West

What I have seen of the love affairs of other people has not led me to regret the deficiency in my experience.

George Bernard Shaw

A woman's guess is much more accurate than a man's certainty.

Rudyard Kipling

The connections between and among women are the most feared, the most problematic, and the most potentially transforming force on the planet.

Adrienne Rich

I do not understand the theory of relativity, but I know my husband, and I know he can be trusted.

Elsa Einstein

Every artist is an unhappy lover.

Iris Murdoch

Men and Women

Try to take for a mate a person of your own neighbourhood.

Hesiod

A woman may very well form a friendship with a man, but for this to endure, it must be assisted by a little physical antipathy.

Friedrich Nietzche

You do not want a woman who will accept your faults, you want one who pretends that you are faultless and one who will caress the hand that strikes her and kiss the lips that lie to her.

George Sand

Marriage is an empty bin. It remains empty unless you put more in than you take out.

H. Jackson Brown

People change and forget to tell each other.

Lillian Hellman

Women rule the world. No man has ever done anything that a woman either hasn't allowed him to do, or encouraged him to do.

Bob Dylan

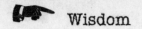

Rarely do great beauty and great virtue dwell together.

Petrarch

God became man, granted. The devil became a woman.

Victor Hugo

The happiest marriages are full of alternative lives, lived in the head, unknown to the partner.

John Bayley

If it was only woman who took man out of Paradise, it is still woman, and woman alone, who can lead him back.

Elbert Hubbard

Good and Evil

The world is not a place where good is rewarded and evil is punished.

Colin Semper

The best is the enemy of the good.

Voltaire

The so-called new morality is too often the old immorality condoned.

Lord Shawcross

There are two kinds of people; those who are always well and those who are always sick. Most of the evils of the world come from the first sort and most of the achievements from the second.

Louis Dudek

The number of malefactors authorises not the crime.

Thomas Fuller

I would rather be the man who bought the Brooklyn Bridge than the man who sold it.

Will Rogers

There are no shortcuts to heaven, only the ordinary ways of ordinary things.

Vincent McNabb

The greatest penalty of evil-doing is to grow into the likeness of a bad man.

Plato

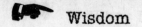

Flee the wicked, even when they are agreeable, instructive, and charming.

Eugene Delacroix

Obscenity is such a tiny kingdom that a single tour covers it completely.

Heywood Broun

Whoever desires to found a state and give it laws must start by assuming that all men are bad and ever ready to display their vicious nature, whenever they many find occasion for it.

Niccolo Machiavelli

The major sin is the sin of being born.

Samuel Beckett

A long habit of not thinking a thing wrong gives it a superficial appearance of being right.

Thomas Paine

Those who flee temptation generally leave a forwarding address.

Lane Olinghouse

The sorrow of knowing that there is evil in the best is far out balanced by the joy of discovering that there is good in the worst.

Austin Riggs

Idleness is the well-spring and root of all vice.

Thomas Becon

Right is right even if nobody does it. Wrong is wrong even if everybody is wrong about it.

G. K. Chesterton

To have a right to do a thing is not at all the same as to be right in doing it.

G. K. Chesterton

In anything it is a mistake to think that one can perform an action or behave in a certain way once and no more. What one does, one will do again, and indeed has probably already done in the distant past.

Cesare Pavese

The evil that men do lives after them;
The good is oft interred with their bones.

William Shakespeare

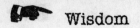

In our era the road to holiness necessarily passes
through the world of action.

Dag Hammarskjôld

Never open the door to a lesser evil, for other and
greater ones invariable slink in after it.

Baltasar Gracian

Morality is a private and costly luxury.

Henry B. Adams

The tendency of man's nature to good is like the
tendency of water to flow downwards.

Mencius

A hurtful act is the transference to others of the
degradation which we bear in ourselves.

Simone Weil

Nobody ever suddenly became depraved.

Juvenal

In matters of conscience, the law of majority has
no place.

Mahatma Gandhi

The essence of immorality is the tendency to make an exception of one's self.

> Jane Addams

Who are the greater criminals – those who sell the instruments of death, or those who buy and use them?

> Robert E. Sherwood

The enemies of the future are always the very nicest people.

> Christopher Morley

Sooner or later, false thinking brings wrong conduct.

> Julian Huxley

Adam was but human – this explains it all. He did not want the apple for the apple's sake, he wanted it only because it was forbidden. The mistake was not forbidding the serpent; then he would have eaten the serpent.

> Mark Twain

All sins are attempts to fill voids.

> Simone Weil

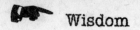

Gossip needn't be false to be evil – there's a lot of truth that shouldn't be passed around.

Frank Clarke

Goodness does not more certainly make men happy than happiness makes them good.

Walter Savage Landor

The highest possible stage in moral culture is when we recognise that we ought to control our thoughts.

Charles Darwin

I walk firmer and more secure up hill than down.

Michel de Montaigne

Man must search for what is right, and let happiness come on its own.

Johann Pestalozzi

Boredom is a vital problem for the moralist, since at least half the sins of mankind are caused by the fear of it.

Bertrand Russell

While forbidden fruit is said to taste sweeter, it usually spoils faster.

Abigail Van Buren

Behind every great fortune there is a crime.

Honoré de Balzac

Wherever a man commits a crime, God finds a witness. Every secret crime has its reporter.

Ralph Waldo Emerson

Remorse is impotence; it will sin again. Only repentance is strong; it can end everything.

Henry Miller

What man have you ever seen who was contented with one crime only?

Juvenal

Why do you necessarily have to be wrong just because a few million people think you are?

Frank Zappa

Everything that used to be a sin is now a disease.

Bill Maher

Dishonesty is like a boomerang. Just when you think all is well, it hits you on the back of the head.

H. Jackson Brown

It is the mark of a good action that it appears inevitable in retrospect.

Robert Louis Stevenson

I came to the conclusion many years ago that almost all crime is due to the repressed desire for aesthetic expression.

Evelyn Waugh

I shot an error in the air,
It's still going everywhere.

Robert Heinlein

Art is an attempt to integrate evil.

Simone de Beauvoir

Saintliness is also a temptation.

Jean Anouilh

Any crooked bookkeeper's books are balanced.

James Ferguson

The accomplished hypocrite does not exercise his skill upon every possible occasion. In all unimportant matters, who is more just, more upright, more candid, more honourable?

Arthur Helps

Goodness does not consist in greatness, but greatness in goodness.

Athenaeus

A man who will steal for me will steal from me.

Theodore Roosevelt

Many are saved from sin by being so inept at it.

Mignon McLaughlin

The greatest slave is not he who is ruled by a despot, great though that evil may be, but one who is in the thrall of his own moral ignorance, selfishness and vice.

Samuel Smiles

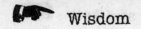

Evil unchecked grows, evil tolerated poisons the whole system.

Jawaharlal Nehru

It is easier to resist at the beginning than at the end.

Leonardo da Vinci

The truth of the matter is that you always know the right thing to do. The hard part is doing it.

Norman Schwarzkopf

Evil is something you recognise immediately you see it: it works through charm.

Brian Masters

Men are qualified for civic liberties in exact proportion to their disposition to put moral chains upon their appetites.

Edmund Burke

Pop music is about stealing pocket money from children.

Ian Anderson

Virtue consists not in abstaining from vice, but in not desiring it.

George Bernard Shaw

There is no such thing as a minor lapse of integrity.

Tom Peters

I believe the moral losses of expediency always far outweigh the temporary gains.

Wendell. Wilkie

Men can heal lust. Angels can heal malice. God alone can cure pride.

John Climacus

The law does not content itself with classifying and punishing crime. It invents crime.

Norman Douglas

No cause is helpless if it is just. Errors, no matter how popular, carry the seeds of their own destruction.

John W. Scoville

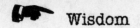

The foundation of all morality is to have done, once and for all, with lying.

Thomas Hardy

Apathy is the glove into which evil slips its hand.

Bodie Thorne

Success is the sole earthly judge of right and wrong.

Adolf Hitler

The greater the wealth, the thicker will be the dirt.

J. K. Galbraith

Remember the weekday to keep it holy.

Elbert Hubbard

No man chooses evil because it is evil; he only mistakes it for happiness, the good he seeks.

Mary Wollstonecraft

He who does not punish evil commands it to be done.

Leonardo da Vinci

Artists are exposed to great temptations; their eyes see paradise before their souls have reached it, and that is a great danger.

Phyllis Bottome

No man has a right to do what he pleases, except when he pleases to do right.

Charles Simmons

Anybody can observe the Sabbath, but making it holy surely takes the rest of the week.

Alice Walker

Our culture resolutely refuses to believe in the real existence of evil, preferring to regard it as a kind of systems breakdown that can be fixed through tinkering.

Walter Wink

Once we assuage our conscience by calling something a 'necessary evil', it begins to look more and more necessary and less and less evil.

Sydney J. Harris

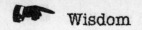

Vice is the sacrifice of the future to the present.

Humbert Wolfe

To see and listen to the wicked is already the beginning of wickedness.

Confucius

The wicked work harder to reach hell than the righteous to reach heaven.

Josh Billings

He that avoideth not small faults, by little and little falleth into greater.

Thomas à Kempis

Conscience is thoroughly well bred and soon leaves off talking to those who don't wish to hear it.

Samuel Butler

Do not wait for extraordinary circumstances to do good; try to use ordinary situations.

Jean Paul Richter

Gluttony is not a secret vice.

Orson Welles

It often happens that, if a lie be believed for only an hour, it has done its work, and there is not further occasion for it.

Jonathan Swift

Sin has many tools, but a lie is the handle that fits them all.

Oliver Wendell Holmes

The road to vice is not only downhill but steep.

Seneca

The confession of evil works is the first beginning of good works.

St Augustine

Don't repent. Stop sinning.

Ken Alstad

Whatever you condemn, you have done yourself.

Georg Groddeck

All men are tempted. There is no man that lives that can't be broken down, provided it is the right temptation, put in the right spot.

Henry Ward Beecher

Sins become more subtle as you grow older. You commit sins of despair rather than lust.

Piers Paul Read

War and Peace

There will be no veterans of World War Three.

Walter Mondale

Men love war because it allows them to look serious — it is the one thing that stops women laughing at them.

John Fowles

When the rich wage war it's the poor who die.

Jean-Paul Sartre

You can no more win a war that you can win an earthquake.

Jeannette Rankin

In wartime, to have a woman as your nurse when seriously injured increased a soldier's chance of recovery by fifty percent.

Eric Taylor

'Peace' remains a mere name for the resting-place between wars.

H. G. Wells

In war the heroes always outnumber the soldiers ten to one.

H. L. Mencken

In battle those who are most afraid are always in most danger.

Catiline

Bullets cannot be recalled. They cannot be uninvented. But they can be taken out of the gun.

Martin Amis

I hate war as only a soldier who has lived it can, only as one who has seen its brutality, its futility, its stupidity.

Dwight D. Eisenhower

Nothing is ever done in this world until men are prepared to kill one another if it is not done.

George Bernard Shaw

Untutored courage is useless in the face of educated bullets.

George Patton

Being a hero is the shortest-lived profession on earth.

Will Rogers

Everything, everything in war is barbaric, but the worst barbarity of war is that it forces men collectively to commit acts against which individually they would revolt with their whole being.

Ellen Key

You cannot shake hands with a clenched fist.

Indira Gandhi

War and Peace

How good bad music and bad reasons sound when we march against an enemy.

Friedrich Nietzsche

The act of creation is older than the act of killing.

Andrei Voznesensky

It is my contention that killing under the cloak of war is nothing but an act of murder.

Albert Einstein

A man may build himself a throne of bayonets, but he cannot sit on it.

W. R. Inge

There never was a good war, nor a bad peace.

Benjamin Franklin

Serious sport has nothing to do with fair play. It is bound up with hatred, jealousy, boastfulness, disregard of all rules and sadistic pleasure in witness violence: in other words it is war minus the shooting.

George Orwell

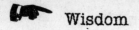

War even in its mildest form, is a perpetual violation of every religion and humanity.

Edward Gibbon

If you strike a child, take care that you strike it in anger, even at the risk of maiming it for life. A blow in cold blood neither can nor should be forgiven.

George Bernard Shaw

The use of force alone is but temporary. It may subdue for a moment; but it does not remove the necessity of subduing again: and a nation is not governed, which is perpetually to be conquered.

Edmund Burke

Non-violence is a flop. The only bigger flop is violence.

Joan Baez

War is capitalism with the gloves off.

Tom Stoppard

If sunbeams were weapons of war we would have had solar energy long ago.

George Porter

Strong men can always afford to be gentle. Only the weak are intent on giving as good as they get.

Elbert Hubbard

I shall never permit myself to sink so low as to hate any man.

Booker T. Washington

Every gun that is made, every warship launched, every rocket fired, signifies in the final sense a theft from those who hunger and are not fed, those who are cold and are not clothed.

Dwight D. Eisenhower

The belief in the possibility of a short decisive war appears to be one of the most ancient and dangerous of human illusions.

Robert Lynd

My centre is giving way, my right is retreating, situation excellent, I am attacking.

Marshal Foch

We prefer to lose because of the ability of the opposition rather than the inability of the referee.

Kenny Dalglish

Nobody ever forgets where he buried the hatchet.

Kin Hubbard

In peace sons bury their fathers and in war the fathers bury their sons.

Francis Bacon

The end result of freedom will always be a dictatorship of the masses. Believe me, behind that word 'freedom' demons lurk.

Bernhard Rust

Only the winners decide what were war crimes.

Gary Wills

War is common to all and strife is justice, and all things come into being and pass away through strife.

Heraclitus

No snowflake in the avalanche ever feels responsible.

Stanislaw Lec

I prefer my people to be loyal out of fear rather than conviction. Convictions can change but fear remains.

Josef Stalin

The notion that disarmament can put a stop to war is contradicted by the nearest dogfight.

George Bernard Shaw

Persecution was at least a sign of personal interest. Tolerance is composed of nine parts of apathy to one of brotherly love.

Frank M. Colby

Although the world is full of suffering it is also full of the overcoming of suffering.

Helen Keller

War will exist until that distant day when the conscientious objector enjoys the same reputation and prestige that the warrior does today.

John F. Kennedy

The enemy is anybody who's going to get you killed, no matter which side he's on.

Joseph Heller

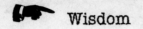

Appeasers believe that if you keep on throwing
steaks to a tiger, the tiger will become a
vegetarian.

Heywood Broun

What do you despise? By this you are truly
known.

Frank Herbert

The nose of the bulldog has been slanted
backwards so that he can breathe without letting
go.

Winston Churchill

War will never cease until babies are born into the
world with larger brains and smaller adrenal
glands.

H. L. Mencken

Enemies are not those who hate us, but rather
those whom we hate.

Dagobert Runes

Treating your adversary with respect is giving him
an advantage to which he is not entitled.

Samuel Johnson

In order to have good soldiers a nation must always be at war.

Napoleon Bonaparte

The weakest link in a chain is the most powerful because it can break the chain.

Stanislaw Lec

Don't hit at all if it is honourably possible to avoid hitting; but never hit soft.

Theodore Roosevelt

A dead man who never caused others to die seldom rates a statue.

Samuel Butler

One of the laws of palaeontology is that an animal which must protect itself with thick armour is degenerate. It is usually a sign that the species is on the road to extinction.

Gertrude Stein

Science and Nature

Growth for the sake of growth is the ideology of the cancer cell.

Edward Abbey

Pollution is nothing but resources we're not using.

Richard Buckminster Fuller

If your theory is found to be against the second law of thermodynamics, I give you no hope; there is nothing for it but to collapse in deepest humiliation.

Arthur Eddington

The question of whether computers can think is just like the question of whether submarines can swim.

Edger Dijkstra

Most of the population of the world has never made a phone call.

Noam Chomsky

What am I interested in? Everything!

Thomas Edison

The hand is the cutting edge of the mind.

Jacob Bronowski

Statistically, the probability of any one of us being here is so small that you'd think the mere fact of existing would keep us all in a contented dazzlement of surprise.

Lewis Thomas

The human race likes to give itself airs. One good volcano can produce more greenhouse gases in a year than the human race has in its entire history.

Ray Bradbury

Animals have these advantages over man; they never hear the clock strike, they die without any idea of death, they have no theologians to instruct them, their last moments are not disturbed by unwelcome and unpleasant ceremonies, their funerals cost them nothing, and no one starts lawsuits over their wills.

Voltaire

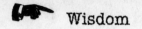

Don't fight forces; use them.

Richard Buckminster Fuller

The most technologically efficient machine that man ever invented is the book.

Northrop Frye

Science can analyse the alternatives of sound and silence that go to make up a piece of music, but it is quite powerless to explain why one piece is an immortal masterpiece and another in similar form is ephemeral rubbish. Science can analyse chemical components of a human being, but give no qualitative account of his personality.

L. A. Strong

You may observe mother instinct at its height in a fond hen sitting on china eggs – instinct but no brains.

Charlotte Gilman

I never did a day's work in my life. It was all fun.

Thomas Edison

Heredity is nothing but stored environment.

Luther Burbank

If at first the idea is not absurd, then there is no hope for it.

Albert Einstein

I just invent, then wait until man comes around to needing what I've invented.

Richard Buckminster Fuller

A hundred times every day I remind myself that my inner and outer life depend on the labours of other men, living and dead, and that I must exert myself in order to give in the same measure as I have received.

Albert Einstein

If we do not permit the earth to produce beauty and joy, it will not produce food either.

Joseph Krutch

Thousands have lived without love, not one without water.

W. H. Auden

The greatest of all inventors is accident.

Mark Twain

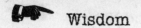

No pessimist ever discovered the secrets of the stars, or sailed to an uncharted land, or opened a new heaven to the human spirit.

Helen Keller

Results! Why, man, I have gotten a lot of results. I know several thousand things that don't work.

Thomas Edison

There is no evil in the atom; only in men's souls.

Adlai Stevenson

The scientist who comes to ask metaphysical questions and turns away from metaphysical answers may be afraid of those answers.

Gregory Zilboorg

Nobody who has ever been on a falling elevator and survived ever again approaches such a conveyance without a fundamentally reduced degree of confidence.

Robert Reno

Those who are not shocked by quantum theory do not understand it.

Niels Bohr

Humour is grit in the evolutionary process.

Heywood Broun

Civilisation is just a temporary failure of entropy.

Christine Nelson

Television is as injurious to the soul as fast food is to the body.

Quentin Crisp

If the stars should appear just one night in a thousand years, how would men believe and adore?

Ralph Waldo Emerson

The sun, the moon and the stars would all have disappeared years ago, had they happened to be within reach of predatory human hands.

Havelock Ellis

I am proud of the fact that I never invented weapons to kill.

Thomas Edison

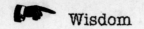

There are no passengers on Spaceship Earth. We are all crew.

Marshall McLuhan

Diseases are the tax on pleasures.

John Ray

Even when all the possible scientific questions have been answered, the problems of life remain completely untouched.

Ludwig Wittgenstein

Many inventions had their birth as a toy.

Eric Heffer

The proliferation of radio and television channels has produced a wilderness of cave-dwellers instead of the promised global village.

Philip Howard

We should always presume the disease to be curable, until its own nature prove it otherwise.

Peter Latham

The universe is like a safe to which there is a combination – but the combination is locked in the safe.

Peter de Vries

Now there is one outstandingly important fact regarding Spaceship Earth, and that is that no instruction book came with it.

Richard Buckminster Fuller

I'm replacing some of the timber used up by my books. Books are just trees with squiggles on them.

Hammond Innes

Intelligence cannot be present without understanding. No computer has any awareness of what it does.

Roger Penrose

Serious people have few ideas. People with ideas are never serious.

Paul Vallely

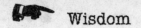

In the mountains the shortest way is from peak to peak: but for that one must have long legs.

Friedrich Nietzsche

The place where we do our scientific work is a place of prayer.

Joseph Needham

Science is really in the business of disproving its current models or changing them to conform to new information. In essence, we are constantly proving our latest ideas wrong.

David Suzuki

A year spent in artificial intelligence is enough to make one believe in God.

Alan J. Perlis

Gardening is an active participation in the deepest mysteries of the universe.

Thomas Berry

The best way to get great ideas is to get lots of ideas and throw the bad ones away.

Charles Thompson

The best way to show that a stick is crooked is not to argue about it, or spend your time trying to straighten it, but to lay a straight stick alongside of it.

Dwight L. Moody

As cruel a weapon as the caveman's club, the chemical barrage has been hurled against the fabric of life.

Rachel Carson

The outcome of Einstein's doubt and befogged speculation about time and space is a cloak which hides the ghastly apparition of atheism.

William Henry O'Connell

The serial number of a human specimen is the face, that accidental and unrepeatable combination of features. It reflects neither character nor soul nor what we call the self.

Milan Kundera

My soul can find no staircase to heaven unless it be through earth's loveliness.

Michelangelo

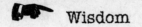

Each success buys only an admission ticket to a more difficult problem.

Henry Kissinger

If a lot of cures are suggested for a disease, it means that the disease is incurable.

Anton Chekhov

The creation of a thousand forests is in one acorn.

Ralph Waldo Emerson

Some of the world's greatest feats were accomplished by people not smart enough to know they were impossible.

Doug Larson

Nothing happens to anybody which he is not fitted by nature to bear.

Marcus Aurelius

Science has 'explained' nothing; the more we know, the more fantastic the world becomes and the profounder the surrounding darkness.

Aldous Huxley

Necessity is the mother of invention, but its father is creativity, and knowledge is the midwife.

Jonathon Schattke

I saw the angel in the marble and carved until I set him free.

Michelangelo

Whatever Nature has in store for mankind, unpleasant as it may be, man must accept, for ignorance is never better than knowledge.

Enrico Fermi

Each of us visits this Earth involuntarily and without an invitation. For me, it is enough to wonder at its secrets.

Albert Einstein

The only thing you will ever be able to say in the so-called 'social' sciences is 'some do, some don't'.

Ernest Rutherford

Every investigation which is guided by principles of Nature fixes its ultimate aim entirely on gratifying the stomach.

Athenaeus

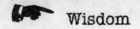

Anyone who has a library and a garden wants for nothing.

Cicero

I like to browse in occult bookshops if for no other reason than to refresh my commitment to science.

Heinz Pagels

There are no atheists in black holes.

Des MacHale

The most incomprehensible fact about the universe is that it is comprehensible.

Albert Einstein

Failure is just Nature's plan to prepare you for great responsibilities.

Napoleon Hill

I am spending delightful afternoons in my gardens, watching everything living around me. As I grow older, I feel everything departing and I love everything with more passion.

Emile Zola

Only the most foolish of mice would hide in a cat's ear. But only the wisest of cats would think to look there.

Scott Love

The secret of flight is this: you have to do it immediately, before your body realises it is defying the laws.

Michael Cunningham

Make it a practice to keep on the lookout for novel and interesting ideas that others have used successfully. Your idea has to be original only in its adaptation to the problem you are working on.

Thomas Edison

Mothers and Fathers

The real measure of your success is one you cannot spend – it's the way your child describes you when talking to a friend.

Martin Baxbaum

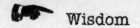

There are fathers who do not love their children;
there is no grandfather who does not adore his
grandson.

Victor Hugo

If people waited to know each other before they
were married, the world wouldn't be so grossly
over-populated.

Somerset Maugham

There are times when parenthood seems nothing
but feeding the mouth that bites you.

Peter de Vries

Mother is far too clever to understand anything
she does not like.

Arnold Bennett

The dark uneasy world of family life – where the
greatest can fail and the humblest succeed.

Randall Jarrell

A sleeping child gives me the impression of a
traveller in a very far country.

Ralph Waldo Emerson

You don't have to deserve your mother's love. You have to deserve your father's. He's more particular.

Robert Frost

Blaming mother is just a negative way of clinging to her still.

Nancy Friday

What a mother sings to the cradle goes all the way down to the coffin.

Henry Ward Beecher

A mother who is really a mother is never free.

Honoré De Balzac

By the time a man realises that maybe his father was right, he usually has a son who thinks he's wrong.

Charles Wadsworth

Every new generation is a fresh invasion of savages.

Hervey Allen

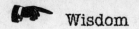

It is easy to become a father, but very difficult to be a father.

Wilhelm Busch

Your children are not your children ... You are the bows from which your children as living arrows are sent forth.

Kahlil Gibran

Every unpunished deliquent has a family of delinquencies.

Herbert Spencer

We bear the world and we make it. There was never a great man who had not a great mother.

Olive Schreiner

You don't really understand human nature unless you know why a child on a merry-go-round will wave at his parents every time around – and why the parents will always wave back.

William Tammeus

Babies are the enemies of the human race.

Isaac Asimov

We don't inherit the earth, we borrow it from our children.

David Brower

We are always too busy for our children; we never give them the time or interest they deserve. We lavish gifts upon them; but the most precious gift – our personal association, which means so much to them – we give grudgingly.

Mark Twain

Home wasn't built in a day.

Jane Ace

Raising children is like making biscuits: it is as easy to raise a big batch as one, while you have your hands in the dough.

E. W. Howe

Every parent is at some time the father of the unreturned prodigal, with nothing to do but keep his house open to hope.

John Ciardi

A happy family is but an earlier heaven.

John Bowring

Art is a jealous mistress, and if a man have a genius for painting, poetry, music, architecture, or philosophy, he makes a bad husband and an ill provider.

Ralph Waldo Emerson

If you want to see what children can do, you must stop giving them things.

Norman Douglas

In communities where men build ships for their own sons to fish or fight from, quality is never a problem.

J. Deville

It is the general rule that all superior men inherit the elements of superiority from their mothers.

Michelet

Few, perhaps, are the children who, after the expiration of some months or years, would sincerely rejoice in the resurrection of their parents.

Edward Gibbon

Likely as not, the child you can do the least with will do the most to make you proud.

Mignon McLaughlin

The proliferation of support groups suggests that too many Americans are growing up in homes that do not contain a grandmother.

Florence King

I loved my mother from the day she died.

Michael Hartnett

Children need love, especially when they do not deserve it.

Harold S. Hubert

Home is heaven for beginners.

Charles H. Parkhurst

The family you come from isn't as important as the one you're going to have.

Ring Lardner

We are all brothers now – all Cains and Abels.

Douglas Jerrold

There was a time when we expected nothing of our children but obedience, as opposed to the present, when we expect everything of them but obedience.

Anatole Broyard

A childish soul not inoculated with compulsory prayer is a soul open to any religious infection.

Alexander Cockburn

If spanking children worked, we would have to do it only once.

Nancy Samalin

Corporal punishment is as humiliating for him who gives it as for him who receives it; it is ineffective besides. Neither shame nor physical pain has any other effect than a hardening one.

Ellen Key

'Honour thy father and thy mother' stands written among the three laws of most revered righteousness.

Aeschylus

A healthy family is sacred territory.

John Lane

You have a wonderful child. Then, when he's thirteen, gremlins carry him away and leave in his place a stranger who gives you not a moment's peace.

Jill Eichenberry

The work will wait while you show the child the rainbow, but the rainbow won't wait while you do the work.

Joan O'Hara

Parents must always get across the idea that 'I love you always, but sometimes I do not love your behaviour'.

Amy Vanderbilt

It was the kiss from my mother that greeted my childish drawing of my baby sister that made me a painter.

Benjamin West

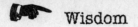

Any individual does not get cancer; a family does.

Terry Williams

No nation has ever prospered in which family life was not held sacred.

W. R. Inge

The family is one of nature's masterpieces.

George Santayana

Give a little love to a child, and you get a great deal back.

John Ruskin

The time not to become a father is eighteen years before a war.

E.B. White

I could not point to any need in childhood as strong as that for a father's protection.

Sigmund Freud

Our love for our children springs from the soul's greatest yearning for immortality.

Plato

I did not become a father because I am fond of children.

Thales

The child is the father of the man.

William Wordsworth

If you want your children to turn out well, spend twice as much time with them as you think you should and half the amount of money.

Esther Selsdon

Show me a man who doesn't let his kids win, and I'll show you a man too hungry for victories.

Hugh O'Neill

A child does not need to be parented. It needs to be mothered and fathered.

Zan Thompson

Why beat your children when the world will do it for you?

Robert Byrne

A child enters your home and for the next twenty years makes so much noise you can hardly stand it. The child departs, leaving the house so silent you think you are going mad.

John Holmes

Any father whose son raises a hand against him is guilty of having produced a son who raised his hand against him.

Charles Pèguy

Christianity and Jesus

Jesus picked up twelve men from the bottom ranks of business and forged them into an organisation that conquered the world.

Bruce Barton

If a man cannot be a Christian where he is, he cannot be a Christian anywhere.

Henry Ward Beecher

I like your Christ, but I do not like your Christians because they are too unlike your Christ.

Mahatma Gandhi

My own commitment is neither to liberalism nor to Marxism, but to a curious idea put about by a carpenter turned dissident in Palestine that the test of our humanity is to be found in how we treat our enemies.

Paul Oestreicher

Capitalism without bankruptcy is like Christianity without hell.

Frank Borman

Preach the Gospel to every creature. Use words if necessary.

St Francis of Assisi

Bach almost persuades me to become a Christian.

Roger Fry

Nobody worries about Christ as long as he can be kept shut up in churches. He is quite safe inside. But there is always trouble if you try and let him out.

Geoffrey Studdert-Kennedy

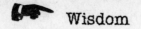

The Christian missionaries did not bring Christ to India; they found Him there.

Alan Richardson

Jesus was the first socialist, the first to seek a better life for mankind.

Mikhail Gorbachev

How could twelve uneducated men, who lived on lakes and rivers and deserts, conceive of such a great enterprise? Their preaching was clearly divinely inspired.

St John Chrysostom

I believe in person to person. Every person is Christ for me, and since there is only one Jesus, that person is the one person in the world at that moment.

Mother Teresa

Jesus promised his disciples three things: that they would be entirely fearless, absurdly happy, and that they would get into trouble.

Russell Maltby

God never built a Christian strong enough to
carry today's duties and tomorrow's anxieties piled
on top of them.

Theodore Cuyler

One is tempted almost to say, that there was more
of Jesus in St. Teresa's little finger than in the whole
of John Knox's body.

Matthew Arnold

Jesus Christ was a man who was completely
innocent, offered himself as a sacrifice for the good
of others, including his enemies, and became the
ransom of the world. It was a perfect act.

Mahatma Gandhi

Religion

My religion consists of a humble admiration of the
illimitable superior spirit who reveals himself in
the slight details we are able to perceive with our
frail and feeble minds.

Albert Einstein

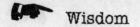

Everything great in the world comes from neurotics. They alone have founded our religions and composed our masterpieces.

Marcel Proust

A Sunday school is a prison in which children do penance for the evil conscience of their parents.

H. L. Mencken

Ye shall know the truth and the truth shall make you mad.

Aldous Huxley

It is important to remember that just because there are crooks, zealots and morons supporting a position, it does not automatically follow that the position is wrong.

Jan D. Walter

The religion that is afraid of science dishonours God and commits suicide.

Ralph Waldo Emerson

The church which is married to the Spirit of its Age will be a widow in the next.

Dean Inge

Sex is the mysticism of materialism and the only possible religion in a materialistic society.

Malcolm Muggeridge

The church is an anvil which has worn out many hammers.

Alexander MacLaren

No religion can be built on force.

George Sand

It is the confession, not the priest, that gives us absolution.

Oscar Wilde

I don't think it is given to any of us to be impertinent to great religions with impunity.

John Le Carré

It is the test of a good religion whether you can make a joke of it.

G. K. Chesterton

Religion is betting your life that there is a God.

Donald Hankey

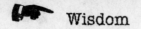

Whenever a man talks loudly against religion –
always suspect that it is not his reason, but his
passions which have got the better of him.

Laurence Sterne

As I take my shoes from the shoemaker, and my
coat from the tailor, so I take my religion from the
priest.

Oliver Goldsmith

A celibate clergy is an especially good idea because
it tends to suppress any hereditary propensity
towards fanaticism.

Carl Sagan

The more I study religion the more I am
convinced that man never worshipped anything
but himself.

Richard Burton

If you have to have a policy manual, publish the
Ten Commandments.

Robert Townsend

There are many religions, but there is only one morality.

John Ruskin

Education and Learning

The mind is its own place and in itself can make a heaven of hell, a hell of heaven.

John Milton

The true secret of giving advice is, after you have honestly given it, to be perfectly indifferent whether it is taken or not and never persist in trying to set people right.

Hannah Smith

A layman knows he has to kick it; an amateur knows where to kick it; a professional knows how hard.

Danny Hillis

Give me a fruitful error any time, full of seeds, bursting with its own corrections. You can keep your sterile truth for yourself.

Vilfredo Pareto

If you give a man a fish, then you have fed him for one day. If you give him a fishing rod then you have fed him for a lifetime. But if you teach him how to make fishing rods, then you have fed the whole village.

Raj Reddy

The object of teaching a child is to enable him to get along without a teacher.

Elbert Hubbard

The best way to have a good idea is to have a lot of ideas.

Linus Pauling

Poetry is language at its most nourishing. It's the breast milk of language.

Robert Crawford

Universities should be safe havens where ruthless examination of realities will not be distorted by the aim to please or inhibited by the risk of displeasure.

Kingman Brewster

Next to being right in this world, the best of all things is to be clearly and definitely wrong.

T. H. Huxley

The most important thing in communication is to hear what isn't being said.

Peter F. Drucker

There's nothing that can help you understand your own beliefs more than trying to explain them to an inquisitive child.

Frank Clark

Education is the best provision for old age.

Aristotle

When you have a public that is literate without being discriminating, they are bound hand and foot.

David Daiches

I have thought about it a great deal, and the more I think the more certain I am that obedience is the gateway through which knowledge, yes and love too, enter the mind of the child.

Annie Sullivan

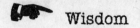

Fear is not a good teacher. The lessons of fear are quickly forgotten.

Mary Bateson

The test of a first-rate intelligence is the ability to hold two opposed ideas in the mind at the same time, and still retain the ability to function.

F. Scott Fitzgerald

It is the province of knowledge to speak and it is the privilege of wisdom to listen.

Oliver Wendell Holmes

Little minds are interested in the extraordinary; great minds in the commonplace.

Elbert Hubbard

The ink of the scholar is more sacred than the blood of the martyr.

Mohammed

Anyone who stops learning is old, whether at twenty or eighty. Anyone who keeps learning stays young. The greatest thing in life is to keep your mind young.

Henry Ford

I touch the future. I teach.

Christa McAuliffe

The man who graduates today and stops learning
tomorrow is uneducated the day after.

Newton D. Baker

School is a building that has four walls – with
tomorrow inside.

Lon Watters

To a person uninstructed in natural history, his
country or seaside stroll is a walk through a gallery
filled with wonderful works of art nine tenths of
which have their faces turned to the wall.

T. H. Huxley

Genius is perseverance in disguise.

Henry Austin

The roots of education are bitter, but the fruit is
sweet.

Aristotle

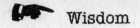

Let early education be a sort of amusement. You will then be better able to find out the natural bent.

Plato

A little learning is a dangerous thing but none at all is fatal.

Roger Bacon

Only the educated are free.

Epictetus

The person who knows 'how' will always have a job. The person who knows 'why' will always be his boss.

Diane Ravitch

An expert is someone who knows some of the worst mistakes that can be made in his subject and how to avoid them.

Werner Heisenberg

Except the blind forces of Nature, nothing moves in this world which is not Greek in its origin.

Henry Maine

A second-hand bookshop is the sign and symbol of a civilised community and the number and quality of these shops give you the exact measure of a city's right to be counted among the great cities of the world.

Walter Murdoch

Be smart, but never show it.

Louis B. Mayer

A critic is at best a waiter at the great table of literature.

Louis Dudek

I would not exchange my early and invincible love of reading for all the treasures of India.

Edward Gibbon

If you would thoroughly know anything, teach it to others.

Tyron Edwards

Advice is like snow; the softer it falls, the longer it dwells upon, and the deeper it sinks into the mind.

Samuel Taylor Coleridge

A specialist is a man who fears the other subjects.

Martin Fischer

Education is the acquisition of the art of the utilisation of knowledge.

A. N. Whitehead

Writers should be read – but neither seen nor heard.

Daphne du Maurier

Genius does not obey the rules – it makes them.

Michael Ghiselin

The height of cleverness is to be able to conceal it.

La Rochefoucauld

Every child is an artist. The problem is how to remain an artist once he grows up.

Pablo Picasso

Everywhere, we learn only from those whom we love.

J. W. von Goethe

Interpretation is the revenge of the intellect upon art.

Susan Sontag

Analysis kills spontaneity. The grain once ground into flour springs and germinates no more.

Henri Amiel

If you cannot read all your books, at any rate handle them, and, as it were, fondle them. Let them fall open where they will. Read on from the first sentence that arrests the eye. Then turn to another. Make a voyage of discovery, taking soundings of uncharted seas.

Winston Churchill

Reading after a certain time diverts the mind too much from its creative pursuits. Any man who reads too much and uses his own brain too little falls into lazy habits of thinking.

Albert Einstein

Genius means little more than the faculty of perceiving in an unhabitual way.

William James

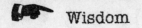

There is no villainy to which education cannot reconcile us.

Anthony Trollope

The writings of the wise are the only riches our posterity cannot squander.

Walter Savage Landor

Disinterested intellectual curiosity is the life-blood of real civilisation.

G. M. Trevelyan

Just as in learning to swim or in learning a language, often toiling on with no apparent result, there comes a day when suddenly we realise we can do it – how we know not; so it is in spiritual matters.

Forbes Robinson

If I understood too clearly what I was doing, where I was going, then I probably wasn't working on anything very interesting.

Peter Carruthers

You hear that winning breeds winning. But no —
winners are bred from losing. They learn that they
don't like it.

Tom Watson

A learned fool is more foolish than an ignorant
fool.

Moliére

She who forms the souls of the young is greater
than any painter or sculptor.

St John Chrysostom

A study of history shows that civilisations that
abandon the quest for knowledge are doomed to
disintegration.

Bernard Lovell

The secret of teaching is to appear to have known
all your life what you learned only yesterday.

John Burns

If you have knowledge, let others light their
candles at it.

Margaret Fuller

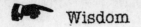

There are no mute inglorious Miltons, save in the hallucinations of poets. The one sound test of a Milton is that he functions as a Milton.

H. L. Mencken

I'm not a teacher: only a fellow traveller of whom you asked the way. I pointed ahead – ahead of myself as well as you.

George Bernard Shaw

Every man has two educations – that which is given to him, and the other, that which he gives to himself. Of the two kinds, the latter is by far the more valuable.

Jean Paul Richter

Learn the fundamentals of the game and stick to them. BandAid remedies never last.

Jack Nicklaus

As knowledge increases, wonder deepens.

Charles Morgan

It is what we think we know already that often prevents us from learning.

Claude Bernard

At every step the child should be allowed to meet the real experiences of life; the thorns should never be plucked from his roses.

Ellen Key

Geniuses all work very hard and are very determined. Intelligence is what we do rather then what we are.

Michael Howe

Knowledge, to become Wisdom, needs Judgement.

Lord Samuel

Education is the systematic, purposeful reconstruction of experience.

John Dewey

There is no real teacher who in practice does not believe in the existence of the soul, or in a magic that acts on it through speech.

Allan Bloom

A teacher affects eternity – he can never tell where his influence stops.

Henry B. Adams

Once we are destined to live out our lives in the prison of our mind, our one duty is to furnish it well.

Peter Ustinov

There must be such a thing as a child with average ability, but you can't find a parent who will admit that it is his child. Start a program for gifted children and every parent demands that his child be enrolled.

Thomas D. Bailey

I owe everything to a system that made me learn by heart till I wept. As a result I have thousands of lines of poetry by heart. I owe everything to this.

George Steiner

I have read little. If I had read as much as other men had, I would have known as little.

Thomas Hobbes

The learning most necessary for a man's life is to unlearn that which is nought.

Francis Bacon

Once in every seven years I burn all my sermons; for it is a shame if I cannot write better sermons now than I did seven years ago.

John Wesley

To make your children capable of honesty is the beginning of education.

John Ruskin

It is an educated barbarian who is the worst; he knows what to destroy.

Helen MacInnes

He who opens a school door closes a prison.

Victor Hugo

You cannot have genius without patience.

Margaret Deland

The kind of world we live in tomorrow depends, not partially, but entirely upon the type and quality of the education of our children today.

Martin Vanbee

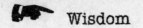

There is precious instruction to be got by finding
we were wrong.

Thomas Carlyle

If there's a book you want to read but it hasn't
been written yet, then you must write it.

Toni Morrison

The mind grows by what it feeds on.

Josiah Holland

Poetry is the opening and closing of a door,
leaving those who look through to guess about
what is seen during a moment.

Carl Sandburg

A man who has not read Homer is like a man who
has not seen the ocean. There is a great object of
which he has no idea.

Walter Bagehot

A wise man speaks because he has something to
say; a fool because he has to say something.

Plato

The chalk marks are transient, the formulae eternal.

S. Weinstein

In the beginner's mind there are many possibilities, but in the expert's mind there are few.

Shunryu Suzuki

Curiosity is one of the most permanent and certain characteristics of a vigorous mind.

Samuel Johnson

Good teaching is one-fourth preparation and three-fourths theatre.

Gail Godwin

'Knowledge is power' is the finest idea ever put into words.

Ernest J. Renan

Genius is the ability to act rightly without precedent – the power to do the right thing the first time.

Elbert Hubbard

The greatest obstacle to discovery is not ignorance
– it is the illusion of knowledge.

Daniel J. Boorstin

Learning is not compulsory. Neither is survival.

W. E. Deming

Education is a private matter between the person
and the world of knowledge and experience, and
has little to do with school or college.

Lillian Smith

Remember, information is not knowledge;
knowledge is not wisdom; wisdom is not truth;
truth is not beauty; beauty is not love; love is not
music; music is the best.

Frank Zappa

Beware of the man of one book.

Thomas Aquinas

It is better to know nothing than what ain't so.

Josh Billings

Failure is the opportunity to begin again more intelligently.

> Henry Ford

Ideas are like rabbits. You get a couple and learn how to handle them, and pretty soon you have a dozen.

> John Steinbeck

The precise statement of any problem is the most important step in its solution.

> Edwin Bliss

Homework should best become a standard fare for all of us for life.

> Tom Peters

The illiterate of the future will not be the person who cannot read. It will be the person who does not know how to learn.

> Alvin Toffler

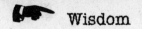

Prayer and Supplication

Almighty God, forgive me for my agnosticism; for I shall try to keep it gentle, not cynical nor a bad influence. And O! If Thou art truly in the heavens, accept my gratitude for all Thy gifts and I shall try to fight the good fight. Amen.

John Gunther

O Lord, if there is a Lord, save my soul, if I have a soul.

Ernest Renan

If Christ himself needed to retire from time to time to the mountain top to pray, lesser men need not be ashamed to acknowledge that necessity.

B. H. Streeter

From silly devotions and sour-faced saints good Lord, deliver us.

St Teresa of Avila

My prayer is, 'Lord, reform thy world, beginning with me'.

Franklin D. Roosevelt

These things, good Lord, that we pray for, give us
Thy grace to labour for.

Thomas More

Don't put people down, unless it's on your prayer
list.

Stan Michalski

There are few men who dare publish to the world
the prayers they make to Almighty God.

Michel de Montaigne

Prayer is not a substitute for work, thinking,
watching, suffering or giving; prayer is a support
for all other efforts.

George Buttrick

Providence gives us the same reply as the soldier
who was begged by a prisoner to spare his life:
'Impossible – though you can ask me for anything
else'.

Ximenes Doudan

Prayer is the slender nerve that moves the muscle
of omnipotence.

Martin Tupper

God insists that we ask, not because He needs to
know our situation, but because we need the
spiritual discipline of asking.

Catherine Marshall

We never ask God to forgive anybody except
where we haven't.

Elbert Hubbard

My Lord, I thank you for having created me.

St Clare of Assisi

Do not pray for easy lives. Pray to be stronger
people. Do not pray for tasks equal to your
powers. Pray for powers equal to your tasks.

Phillip Brooks

Common people do not pray; they only beg.

George Bernard Shaw

Give me, Lord, neither poverty nor riches.

William Cobbett

One single grateful thought raised to heaven is the most perfect prayer.

G. E. Lessing

Thou, O God, dost sell us all good things at the price of labour.

Leonardo da Vinci

Prayer should be the key of the day and the lock of the night.

Thomas Fuller

If this obstacle is from Thee, Lord, I accept it; but if it is from Satan, I refuse him and all his works in the name of Calvary.

Isobel Kuhn

The Fates are not quite obdurate; they have a grim, sardonic way of granting those who supplicate the thing they wanted yesterday.

Roselle Montgomery

Often when I pray I wonder if I am not posting letters to a non-existent address.

C.S. Lewis

There is nothing that makes us love a man so
much as praying for him.

William Law

Prayer is the central phenomenon of religion, the
very hearthstone of all piety.

Franz Heiler

I pray not for a lighter load but for a stronger back.

Phillip Brooks

Faith and Belief

The witch doctor succeeds for the same reason all
the rest of us succeed. Each patient carries his own
doctor inside him. They come to us not knowing
that truth. We are best when we give the doctor
who resides within each patient a chance to go to
work.

Albert Schweitzer

There is a budding morrow in midnight.

John Keats

A thief believes everybody steals.

E. W. Howe

Everyone has talent. What is rare is the courage to follow the talent to the dark place where it leads.

Erica Jong

Poverty of goods is easily cured; poverty of soul impossible.

Michel de Montaigne

The future belongs to those who believe in the beauty of their dreams.

Eleanor Roosevelt

Above all things, never be afraid. The enemy who forces you to retreat is himself afraid of you at that very moment.

André Maurois

You are not free until you've been made captive by supreme belief.

Marianne Moore

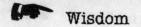

If a million people believe a foolish thing, it is still a foolish thing.

Anatole France

Dreams are the soul's pantry. Keep it well stocked and your soul will never hunger.

Shirley Feeney

There lives more faith in honest doubt, believe me, than in half the creeds.

Alfred Tennyson

An idea isn't responsible for the people who believe it.

Don Marquis

Obsessed by a fairy tale, we spend our lives searching for a magic door and a lost kingdom.

Eugene O'Neill

I have good hope that there is something after death.

Plato

There is no curing a sick man who believes himself to be in health.

Frederic Amiel

Never look back unless you are planning to go that way.

Henry D. Thoreau

One of the most dangerous forms of human error is forgetting what one is trying to achieve.

Paul Nitze

Even doubtful accusations leave a stain behind them.

Thomas Fuller

I could not say I believe. I know! I have had the experience of being gripped by something that is stronger than myself, something that people call God.

Carl Jung

To have doubted one's own first principles is the mark of a civilised man.

Oliver Wendell Holmes

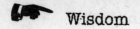

Every man has a right to be wrong in his opinions.
But no man has a right to be wrong in his facts.

Bernard Baruch

Whatever you do, or dream you can do, begin it.
Boldness has genius, power and magic in it. Begin
it now.

J. W. von Goethe

People who want milk should not seat themselves
on a stool in the middle of a field in the hope that
the cow will back up to them.

Elbert Hubbard

In matters of style, swim with the current; in
matters of principle, stand like a rock.

Thomas Jefferson

We can believe what we choose, but we are
answerable for what we choose to believe.

John Henry Newman

The worst vice of a fanatic is his sincerity.

Oscar Wilde

The world breaks everyone and afterwards many are strong at the broken places.

Ernest Hemingway

Obstacles are what you see when you take your eyes off the goal line.

Vince Lombardi

The block of granite which is an obstacle in the pathway of the weak, becomes a stepping-stone in the pathway of the strong.

Thomas Carlyle

I believe in God like I believe in the sun. Not just because I see it, but because I can see everything else.

C.S. Lewis

The only people who are never converted to spiritualism are conjurers.

George Orwell

Commitment is healthiest when it is not without doubt but in spite of doubt.

Rollo May

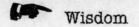

Man may certainly keep on lying (and does so) but he cannot make a truth falsehood.

Karl Barth

Men willingly believe what they wish.

Julius Caesar

Most of the change we think we see in life is due to truths being in and out of fashion.

Robert Frost

In matters of conscience, the law of the majority has no place.

Mahatma Gandhi

There are three classes of people. Those who see; those who see when they are shown; those who do not see.

Leonardo da Vinci

To believe your own thought, to believe that what is true for you in your private heart is true for all men – that is genius.

Ralph Waldo Emerson

Religion masks the face of God.

> Martin Buber

No one can be an unbeliever nowadays. The Christian Apologists have left one nothing to disbelieve.

> Saki

I know you are an atheist, but won't you accept an old man's blessing?

> Pope John XXIII

Whether you believe you can, or whether you believe you can't, you're absolutely right.

> Henry Ford

Every exit is an entrance somewhere else.

> Tom Stoppard

Let nothing disturb thee, Let nothing dismay thee, All things pass; God never changes.

> St Teresa of Avila

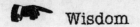

When you are right, you have a moral duty to impose your will upon anyone who disagrees with you.

Tomas de Torquemada

It may offend us to hear our own thoughts expressed by others; we are not sure enough of their souls.

Jean Rostand

An atheist is someone who believes himself an accident.

Francis Thompson

The only tyrant I accept in this world is the still voice within.

Mahatma Gandhi

Lies written in ink cannot obscure a truth written in blood.

Lu Xun

Accept the things to which fate binds you, and love the people with whom fate brings you together, but do so with all your heart.

Marcus Aurelius

Man prefers to believe what he prefers to be true.

Francis Bacon

We are not human beings on a spiritual journey.
We are spiritual beings on a human journey.

Stephen Covey

The pagan soul is like a bird fluttering about in the
gloom, beating against the windows when all the
time the doors are open to the air and sun.

Evelyn Waugh

Do not despair, one of the thieves was saved; do
not presume, one of the thieves was damned.

St Augustine

A casual stroll through a lunatic asylum shows that
faith does not prove anything.

Friedrich Nietzsche

Simple and sincere minds are never more than half
mistaken.

Joseph Joubert

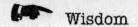

A young man who wishes to remain a sound atheist cannot be too careful of his reading.

C. S. Lewis

Philosophy and Thought

What is your aim in philosophy? To show the fly the way out of the fly-bottle.

Ludwig Wittgenstein

If anything goes badly, I did it. If anything goes semi-well, then we did it. If anything goes really well, then you did it. That's all it takes to get people to win football games.

Paul Bryant

Facts do not cease to exist because they are ignored.

Aldous Huxley

Life is unfair but remember: sometimes it is unfair in your favour.

Peter Ustinov

The most important thing in an argument, next to being right, is to leave an escape hatch for your opponent, so that he can gracefully swing over to your side without too much apparent loss of face.

Sydney J. Harris

Every maybe has a wife called maybe not.

Charlie Chan

There are no whole truths; all truths are half-truths. It is trying to treat them as whole truths that plays the devil.

A. N. Whitehead

Rumour travels faster, but it doesn't stay put as long as truth.

Will Rogers

There are some things so serious that you have to laugh at them.

Niels Bohr

If I am not for myself, who will be for me?
If I am only for myself, who am I?
If not now, when?

Pirke Avoth

Every difficulty slurred over will be a ghost to disturb your repose later on.

Frédéric Chopin

One cannot collect all the beautiful shells on the beach.

Anne Lindbergh

Obstinacy is the will forcing itself into the place of the intellect.

Arthur Schopenhauer

Happiness is beneficial for the body but it is grief that develops the powers of the mind.

Marcel Proust

We are like sailors who must rebuild their ship on the open sea, never able to dismantle it, in dry dock and to reconstruct it there out of the best materials.

Otto Neurath

The drop of rain makes a hole in the stone, not by violence, but by falling often.

Hugh Latimer

The answers are always inside the problem, not outside.

Marshall McLuhan

Wisdom consists of the anticipation of consequences.

Norman Cousins

Everything has two handles, one by which it may be borne, the other by which it may not.

Epictetus

Unless your ideas are ridiculed by the experts they are worth nothing.

Reg Revans

Coincidences are spiritual puns.

G. K. Chesterton

The past is at least secure.

Daniel Webster

Facts do not cease to exist because they are ignored.

Aldous Huxley

Hang ideas! They are tramps, vagabonds, knocking at the back door of your mind, each taking a little of your substance, each carrying away some crumb of that belief in a few simple notions you must cling to if you want to live decently and would like to die easy.

Joseph Conrad

Wisdom never kicks at the iron walls it cannot bring down.

Olive Schreiner

Humour is reason gone mad.

Groucho Marx

Truth gets well if she is run over by a locomotive, while Error dies of lockjaw if she scratches a finger.

Oliver Wendell Holmes

Nothing can keep an argument going like two people who aren't sure what they're arguing about.

O. A. Battista

Mediocre people have an answer to everything and are astounded at nothing.

Eugene Delacroix

Those who love something passionately are more likely to be right than those who don't.

Yehudi Menuhin

A little philosophy carries a man from God, but a great deal brings him back again.

Bathsua Makin

If you don't know, why ask?

John Cage

Our main business is not to see what lies dimly in the distance, but to do what lies clearly at hand.

Thomas Carlyle

When I give food to the poor, they call me a saint. When I ask why the poor have no food, they call me a communist.

Dom. Helder Camara

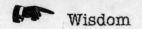

The power of accurate observation is commonly called cynicism by those who have not got it.

George Bernard Shaw

If we don't believe in freedom of expression for people we despise, we don't believe in it at all.

Noam Chomsky

Time is the soul of this world.

Pythagoras

Everything you imagine is real.

Pablo Picasso

There is nothing I like less than bad arguments for a view that I hold dear.

Daniel Dennett

The man who sees both sides of a question is a man who sees absolutely nothing at all.

Oscar Wilde

The moment you think you understand a great work of art, it's dead for you.

Robert Wilson

You cannot fatten a pig on market day.

John Howard

Truth sits upon the lips of dying men.

Matthew Arnold

Truth does not change because it is, or is not,
believed by a majority of the people.

Guido Bruno

I will no more believe that the universe was
formed by a fortuitous concourse of atoms, than
that the accidental jumbling of the alphabet would
fall into a most ingenious treatise of philosophy.

Jonathan Swift

Every violation of truth is not only a sort of
suicide in the liar, but is a stab at the health of
human society.

Ralph Waldo Emerson

If you wish to remove avarice, you must first
remove its mother, luxury.

Cicero

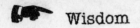

Nothing is so good as it seems beforehand.

George Eliot

You can sway a thousand men by appealing to their prejudices quicker than you can convince one man by logic.

Robert Heinlein

Distinction is the consequence, never the object, of a great mind.

George Allston

An object in possession seldom retains the same charm that it had in pursuit.

Pliny the Younger

Truth which is merely told is quick to be forgotten; truth which is discovered lasts a lifetime.

William Barclay

Prejudice is the child of ignorance.

William Hazlitt

Tradition is the illusion of permanence.

Woody Allen

The world we have made, as a result of the level of thinking we have done thus far, creates problems we cannot solve at the same level of thinking at which we created them.

Albert Einstein

Sometimes one pays most for the things one gets for nothing.

Albert Einstein

In our infinite ignorance, we are all equal.

Karl Popper

Inspiration could be called inhaling the memory of an act never experienced.

Ned Rorem

All looks yellow to the jaundiced eye.

Alexander Pope

What is not good for the beehive cannot be good for the bees.

Marcus Aurelius

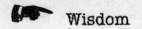

It takes two to communicate truth – one to speak and the other to hear.

Henry D. Thoreau

An essential aspect of creativity is not being afraid to fail.

Edwin Land

The future? Like unwritten books and unborn children, you don't talk about it.

Dietrich Fischer-Dieskeau

I reject the philosophy that if you eliminate the impossible, whatever remains, no matter how improbably, must be the truth. The impossible often has a kind of integrity which the merely improbable lacks.

Douglas Adams

It is a bad plan that admits of no modification.

Publilius Syrus

You are never given a wish without also being given the power to make it come true. You may have to work for it, however.

Richard Bach

Don't worry about people stealing your ideas. If your ideas are any good, you'll have to ram them down people's throats.

Howard Aiken

Truth is not hard to kill and a lie well told is immortal.

Mark Twain

The truth is often a terrible weapon of aggression. It is possible to lie, and even to murder, with the truth.

Alfred Adler

The most exquisite folly is made of wisdom spun too fine.

Benjamin Franklin

Believe those who are seeking the truth. Doubt those who say they have found it.

André Gide

There are no chaste minds. Minds copulate whenever they meet.

Eric Heffer

When we are tired, we are attacked by ideas we conquered long ago.

Friedrich Nietzsche

A wise man ought to realise that his health is his most reliable possession.

Hippocrates

Nagging is the repetition of unpalatable truths.

Edith Summerskill

Do not go where the path may lead, go instead where there is no path and leave a trail.

Ralph Waldo Emerson

The deepest principle of human nature is the craving to be appreciated.

William James

All rising to great places is by a winding stair.

Francis Bacon

Everybody has a degree in hindsight.

Wallace Mercer

The longer the excuse, the less likely it's the truth.

Robert Half

Honesty is the first chapter in the book of wisdom.

Thomas Jefferson

I think, therefore I still am.

Elliot Priest

The lack of meaning in life is a soul-sickness whose full extent and full import our age has not as yet begun to comprehend.

Carl Jung

Time is like the race of a man with a wooden leg after a horse.

Tom Paine

A lot of disappointed people have been left standing on the street corner waiting for the bus marked Perfection.

Donald Kennedy

Bad things are not the worst things that can happen to us. Nothing is the worst thing that can happen to us.

Richard Bach

If you are afraid of being lonely, don't try to be right.

Jules Renard

Know all and you will forgive all.

Thomas à Kempis

Nothing is too wonderful to be true.

Michael Faraday

Knowledge is power.

Francis Bacon

Anyone can hold the helm when the sea is calm.

Publilius Syrus

To love truth is the principal part of human perfection in this world, and the seedplot of all other virtues.

John Locke

A good reputation is more valuable than money.

Publilius Syrus

In order to sew we must first have a knot in the thread.

Sôren Kierkegaard

Politics and Power

One of the penalties for refusing to participate in politics is that you end up being governed by your inferiors.

Plato

Monarchy is the gold filling in the mouth of decay.

John Osborne

Dictators who ride to and fro on tigers dare not dismount.

Winston Churchill

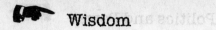

The more corrupt the state, the more numerous the laws.

Tacitus

Democracy is four wolves and a lamb, voting on what to have for lunch.

Wilma Brown

Every government is run by liars and nothing they say should be believed.

I.F. Stone

I start with the premise that the function of leadership is to produce more leaders not more followers.

Ralph Nader

I believe there are more instances of the abridgement of the freedom of the people by gradual and silent encroachment of those in power than by violent and sudden usurpations.

James Madison

Nationalism is absolutely prehistoric.

Peter Ustinov

Revolutions have never lightened the burden of tyranny, they have only shifted it to another shoulder.

George Bernard Shaw

Let us call capital punishment by the name which, for lack of any other nobility, will at least give the nobility of truth, and let us recognise if for what it essentially is: a revenge.

Albert Camus

You cannot adopt politics as a profession and remain honest.

Louis Howe

Never wait, just vote for the least imbecile of the lot and continue griping and create whatever microcosm of perfection you can in your own life.

André Monestier

Always remember that the soundest way to progress in any organisation is to help the man ahead of you to get promoted.

Leon Hamaker

Authority has always attracted the lowest elements in the human race. All through history, mankind has been bullied by scum. Each government is a parliament of whores. The trouble is, in a democracy, the whores are us.

P. J. O'Rourke

Communism is fascism with a human face.

Susan Sontag

Capital punishment in my view achieved nothing except revenge.

Albert Pierrepoint

Fascism is Capitalism plus Murder.

Upton Sinclair

There are two freedoms – the false where a man is free to do what he likes; the true where a man is free to do what he ought.

Charles Kingsley

Whenever a man has cast a longing eye on office, a rottenness begins in his conduct.

Thomas Jefferson

The short memory of voters is what keeps politicians in office.

> Will Rogers

Force is all-conquering but its victories are short-lived.

> Abraham Lincoln

It is dangerous to be right when the government is wrong.

> Voltaire

One of the tests of leadership is the ability to recognise a problem before it is an emergency.

> Arnold Glasow

The modern conservative is engaged in one of man's oldest exercises in moral philosophy; that is the search for a superior moral justification for selfishness.

> J. K. Galbraith

When you see a rattlesnake poised to strike you, you do not wait until he has struck before you crush him.

Franklin D. Roosevelt

Politics is the art of preventing people from becoming involved in affairs which concern them.

Paul Valéry

Ask a man for whom he will vote and he will probably tell you. Ask him why and vagueness is all.

Bernard Levin

The more I study the world, the more I am convinced of the inability of brute force to create anything durable.

Napoleon Bonaparte

So long as men worship the Caesars and Napoleons, Caesars and Napoleons will arise to make them miserable.

Aldous Huxley

Nothing is politically right which is morally wrong.

Daniel O'Connell

In every age the vilest specimens of human nature are to be found among demagogues.

Thomas Babington Macaulay

Freedom is when one hears the bell at seven o'clock in the morning and knows it is the milkman and not the Gestapo.

Georges Bidault

The one pervading evil of democracy is the tyranny of the majority.

John Dahlberg

Thomas Cromwell established the principle that Parliament could condemn a man to death for treason without hearing him in his defence. He was himself the first victim of this measure.

Taswell Langmead

The higher the vote any government wins in an election the more tyrannical it is.

Charles Krauthammer

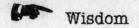

The most dangerous follower is he whose defection would destroy the whole party: that is to say, the best follower.

Friedrich Nietzsche

No one who has not sat in prison knows what the State is like.

Leo Tolstoy

The spirit of reform has been too much concerned with private 'rights', and not enough concerned with the public order that makes them possible.

Roger Scruton

Democracy is supposed to give you the feeling of choice like Painkiller X and Painkiller Y. But they're both just aspirin.

Gore Vidal

The final test of a leader is that he leaves behind him in other men the conviction and the will to carry on.

Walter Lippmann

I have heard many arguments which influenced my opinion but never one which influenced my vote.

James Ferguson

To me judges seem the well paid watch-dogs of Capitalism making things safe and easy for the devil Mammon.

Maud Gonne

The main dangers in this life are the people who want to change everything, or nothing.

Nancy Astor

Revolutionary movements attract those who are not good enough for established institutions as well as those who are too good for them.

George Bernard Shaw

There are only two barriers to megalomania in public life: intelligence and a sense of humour.

Dan Binchy

In politics, as on the sick bed, people toss from side to side, thinking they will be more comfortable.

J. W. Von Goethe

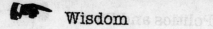

In politics, the plural of conscience is too often conspiracy.

Charles Stewart Parnell

If liberty means anything at all, it means the right to tell people what they do not want to hear.

George Orwell

Freedom is the right to be wrong, not the right to do wrong.

John Diefenbaker

Feelings and Emotions

A man can live for three days without water but not one without poetry.

Oscar Wilde

We crucify ourselves between two thieves; regret for yesterday and fear of tomorrow.

Fulton Oursler

Boredom is rage spread thin.

Thomas Tickell

There is a road from the eye to the heart that does not go through the intellect.

G. K. Chesterton

Human happiness is a stock that doubles every year.

Ira Cobleigh

The three most beautiful words in the English language are 'It is benign'.

Woody Allen

Pain and suffering are inevitable in our lives, but misery is an option.

Chip Beck

Newspapers always excite curiosity. No one ever lays one down without a feeling of disappointment.

Charles Lamb

Music is the only cheap unpunished rapture on earth.

Sydney Smith

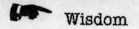

One should either be sad or joyful. Contentment is a warm sty for eaters and sleepers.

Eugene O'Neill

Love knows not depth till the hour of separation.

Kahlil Gibran

There are only two emotions on a plane: boredom and terror.

Orson Welles

Grief is the agony of an instant; the indulgence of grief the blunder of a lifetime.

Benjamin Disraeli

The wretched have no compassion.

Samuel Johnson

When one door closes another door opens; but we so often look so long and so regretfully upon the closed door, that we do not see the ones which open for us.

Alexander Graham Bell

No one can explain how the notes of a Mozart melody, or the folds of a piece of Titian's drapery, produce their essential effects. If you do not feel it, no one can by reasoning make you feel it.

John Ruskin

Groans and complaints are very well for those who are to mourn but a little while; but a sorrow that is to last for a life will not be violent or romantic.

Eva Maria Garrick

Look at everything as though you were seeing it either for the first or last time. Then your time on earth will be filled with glory.

Betty Smith

It is neither wealth nor splendour, but tranquillity and occupation, which give happiness.

Thomas Jefferson

The least pain in our little finger gives us more concern and uneasiness than the destruction of millions of our fellow beings.

William Hazlitt

In the long run the pessimist may be right, but the optimist has a better time on the trip.

Daniel L. Reardon

Loneliness is to endure the presence of one who does not understand.

Elbert Hubbard

Enjoyment is not a goal; it is a feeling that accompanies important ongoing activity.

Paul Goodman

Remember there is nothing stable in human affairs; therefore avoid undue elation in prosperity or undue depression in adversity.

Socrates

To be trusted is a greater compliment than to be loved.

George MacDonald

Courage is a mastery of fear – not absence of fear.

Mark Twain

A man who values a good night's rest will not lie down with enmity in his heart, if he can help it.

Laurence Sterne

Anxiety is a thin stream of fear trickling through the mind. If encouraged, it cuts a channel into which all other thoughts are drained.

Arthur Roche

Remember happiness is a way of travel, not a destination.

Roy Goodman

After playing Chopin, I feel as if I had been weeping over sins that I had never committed.

Oscar Wilde

There is another man within me that is angry with me.

C.S. Lewis

It is better to be feared than loved, if you cannot be both.

Niccolo Machiavelli

If we could read the secret history of our enemies, we should find in each man's life sorrow and suffering enough to disarm all hostility.

Henry Wadsworth Longfellow

Anger is a symptom, a way of cloaking and expressing feelings too awful to experience directly – hurt, bitterness, grief and, most of all, fear.

Joan Rivers

For what human ill does not dawn seem to be an alleviation?

Oscar Wilde

Guilt is the mafia of the mind.

Bob Mandel

A man who is not afraid of the sea will soon be drowned.

J. M. Synge

Half of our difficulties are imaginary and if we keep quiet about them they will disappear.

Robert Lynd

There are many things in your heart you can never tell to another person. They are you, your private joys and sorrows, and you can never tell them. You cheapen yourself, the inside of yourself when you tell them.

Greta Garbo

Sticks and stones may break our bones, but words will break our hearts.

Robert Fulghum

Ecstasy cannot last, but it can carve a channel for something lasting.

E. M. Forster

Love, like fortune, turns upon a wheel and is very much given to rising and falling.

John Vanbrugh

Courage is just fear that has said its prayers.

Dorothy Bernard

If only we'd stop trying to be happy, we could have a pretty good time.

Willard R. Espy

Success is getting what you want. Happiness is
liking what you get.

H. Jackson Brown

It is not work that kills men; it is worry. Work is
healthy; you can hardly put more upon a man than
he can bear. Worry is rust upon the blade. It is not
the revolution that destroys the machinery, but the
friction.

Henry Ward Beecher

There is a law in human nature which draws us to
be like what we passionately condemn.

George Russell

If you have a number of disagreeable duties to
perform, always do the most disagreeable first.

Josiah Quincy

Isn't it strange that we talk least about the things
we think about most?

Charles A. Lindbergh

The formula for complete happiness is to be very
busy with the unimportant.

Edward Newton

It is often hard to bear the tears that we ourselves have created.

Marcel Proust

It is a mistake for a sculptor or a painter to speak or write very often about his job. It releases tension needed for his work.

Henry Moore

When people hear good music, it makes them homesick for something they never had, and never will have.

E. W. Howe

Hatred is self-punishment.

Hosea Ballou

The best love affairs are those we never had.

Norman Lindsay

Every creator painfully experiences the chasm between his inner vision and its ultimate expression.

Isaac Bashevis Singer

Hatred is the coward's revenge for being intimidated.

George Bernard Shaw

The only thing money gives is the freedom of not worrying about money.

Johnny Carson

There is only one innate error, and that is that we are here in order to be happy.

Arthur Schopenhauer

A good scare is worth more to a man than good advice.

E. W. Howe

Anxiety is fear of one's self.

Wilhelm Stekel

No dyspeptic can have a sane outlook on life.

William Osler

A man who fears suffering is already suffering from what he fears.

Michel de Montaigne

Courage is fear holding on a minute longer.

George Patton

Laughter has no foreign accent.

Paul Lowney

Happiness is just an illusion caused by the
temporary absence of reality.

Desmond Cleary

Jealousy is invariable a symptom of neurotic
insecurity.

Robert Heinlein

Office jobs are physically easier, but the worker
takes home worries instead of an aching back.

Horner Bigart

Never mind your happiness; do your duty.

Will Durant

The competitive advantage of IBM's Deep Blue
chess computer is that it has no fear.

Yasser Sierawan

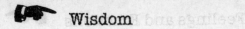

Beware of the people you've been kind to.

Alan Marshall

He alone is great and happy who requires neither
to command nor to obey in order to secure his
being of some importance in this world.

J.W. von Goethe

Forgiveness is the key to action and freedom.

Hannah Arendt

Sadness has an appetite that no misfortune can
satisfy.

E. M. Cioran

There are moments when everything goes well;
don't be frightened – it won't last.

Jules Renard

Those who do not know how to weep with their
whole heart, don't know how to laugh either.

Golda Meir

It is an old mistake, calling desires beliefs.

John Henderson

Anxiety is love's greatest killer. It makes others feel as you might when a drowning man holds onto you. You want to save him, but you know he will strangle you with his panic.

Anais Nin

Nothing in life is to be feared. It is only to be understood.

Marie Curie

Every genuinely benevolent person loathes almsgiving and mendicity.

George Bernard Shaw

Discontent is the first step in the progress of a man or a nation.

Oscar Wilde

To be able to say how much love, is to love but little.

Petrarch

The price of hating other human beings is loving oneself less.

Eldridge Cleaver

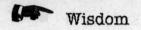

No man can be brave who thinks pain the greatest
evil, nor temperate, who considers pleasure the
highest good.

Cicero

Pity is but a short-lived passion.

Oliver Goldsmith

When someone abuses me I can defend myself;
against praise I am defenceless.

Sigmund Freud

Self-love seems so often unrequited.

Anthony Powell

Impotent hatred is the most horrid of all
emotions; one should hate nobody whom one
cannot destroy.

J.W. von Goethe

The bourgeois prefers comfort to pleasure,
convenience to liberty, and a pleasant temperature
to the deathly inner consuming fire.

Hermann Hesse

The lamentable phrase 'the pursuit of happiness' is responsible for a good part of the ills and miseries of the modern world.

Malcolm Muggeridge

Sadness is almost never anything but a form of fatigue.

André Gide

If the other person injures you, you may forget the injury; but if you injure him you will always remember.

Kahlil Gibran

Anyone who hasn't experienced the ecstasy of betrayal knows nothing about ecstasy at all.

Jean Genet

Fearing the worst is a quality rather than a failing. 'Paranoia' and 'pessimism' are often confused with 'realism'.

Grace Bradberry

Few people can be happy unless they hate some other person, nation or creed.

Bertrand Russell

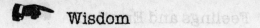

He who has not forgiven an enemy has not yet tasted one of the most sublime enjoyments of life.

Johann Lavater

Happiness is seldom found by those who seek it, and never by those who seek it for themselves.

F. Emerson Andrews

The hunger for love is much more difficult to remove than the hunger for bread.

Mother Teresa

Many a man has become greater, in spite of, as well as because of, disaster.

Eric Liddell

Curiosity will conquer fear even more than bravery will.

James Stephens

To hate fatigues.

Jean Rostand

Anger, used, does not destroy. Hatred does.

Audre Lorde

Develop an infallible technique and then place yourself at the mercy of inspiration.

Ralph Rapson

A man will renounce any pleasures you like but he will not give up his suffering.

George Gurdjieff

Why should you be happy? Do your work.

Colette

The best way to be thankful is to use the goods the gods provide you with.

Anthony Trollope

Until the day of his death, no man can be sure of his courage.

Jean Anouilh

Happiness is something that comes into our lives through doors we don't even remember leaving open.

Rose Lane

It's spring fever — you don't know quite what it is
you want, but it fairly makes your heart ache, you
want it so.

Mark Twain

I hate victims who respect their executioners.

Jean-Paul Sartre

Where there is great love there are always miracles.

Willa Cather

Happiness is a by-product of an effort to make
someone else happy.

Gretta Palmer

Fear is the tax that conscience pays to guilt.

George Sewell

Avarice increases with the increasing pile of gold.

Juvenal

Even the greatest of men cannot rejoice in a
friend's triumph without envy.

Frank Pittman

In anger, you look ten years older.

> Hedda Hopper

Only the brave know to forgive. A coward never forgives; it is not in his nature.

> Laurence Sterne

Lovers of themselves have no rivals.

> Cicero

To forgive is human, to forget is divine.

> James Grand

When a deep injury is done to us, we never recover until we forgive.

> Alan Paton

Many promising reconciliations have broken down because, while both parties come prepared to forgive, neither party came prepared to be forgiven.

> Charles Williams

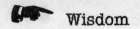

Bigotry may be roughly defined as the anger of men who have no opinions.

G. K. Chesterton

Happiness in intelligent people is the rarest thing I know.

Ernest Hemingway

Nothing is more costly, nothing is more sterile than vengeance.

Winston Churchill

Shyness is egotism out of its depth.

Penelope Keith

To love is to be vulnerable.

C. S. Lewis

There's nothing I'm afraid of like scared people.

Robert Frost

Avoiding danger is no safer in the long run than outright exposure. The fearful are caught as often as the bold.

Helen Keller

Anger repressed can poison a relationship as surely as the cruellest words.

Joyce Brothers

The continuance of anger is hatred.

Frances Quarles

The magic of first love is our ignorance that it can ever end.

Benjamin Disraeli

When the future hinges on the next words that are said, don't let logic interfere, believe your heart instead.

Philip Robinson

Those who have the courage to love should have the courage to suffer.

Anthony Trollope

In the dim background of our mind we know what we ought to be doing but somehow we cannot start.

William James

Silent gratitude is not much use to anyone.

George Bernard Shaw

Some have been thought brave because they were afraid to run away.

Thomas Fuller

In life, pain is inevitable, but suffering is optional.

Hedy Schleifer

Today I bent the truth to be kind, and I have no regret, for I am far surer of what is kind that I am of what is true.

Robert Brault

Rudeness is the weak man's imitation of strength.

Eric Heffer

When people do not respect us we are sharply offended; yet deep down in his heart no man much respects himself.

Mark Twain

If you think you ought to be richer, then you will always feel poor.

Bernard Ingham

There are things so deeply personal that they can be revealed only to strangers.

Richard Rodriguez

Love is a fruit in season at all times, and within reach of every hand.

Mother Teresa

We can make ourselves miserable or we can make ourselves strong. The amount of work is the same.

Carlos Castaneda

False modesty is a sign of ill breeding.

Somerset Maugham

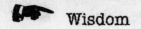

Friendship and Society

It is impossible that a man who is false to his friends and neighbours should be true to the public.

George Berkeley

Friendship is love without his wings.

Lord Byron

A false friend is more dangerous than an open enemy.

Francis Bacon

Artificial manners vanish the moment the natural passions are touched.

Maria Edgeworth

Love comes from blindness; friendship comes from knowledge.

Bussy-Rabutin

As well as loving your enemies, treat your friends a little better.

Milton Friedman

The space in a needle's eye is sufficient for two friends, but the whole world is scarcely big enough to hold two enemies.

Solomon Gabirol

Love your neighbour, yet pull not down your hedge.

George Herbert

It takes a long time to grow an old friend.

John Leonard

Nine out of every ten people improve on acquaintance.

Frank Swinnerton

There is no such thing as conversation. It is an illusion. There are intersecting monologues, that is all.

Rebecca West

Do not fear when your enemies criticise you.
Beware when they applaud.

Vo Dong Giang

In every tyrant's heart there springs in the end this
poison, that he cannot trust a friend.

Aeschylus

The easiest kind of relationship for me is with ten
thousand people. The hardest is with one.

Joan Baez

How shall we expect charity towards others, when
we are uncharitable to ourselves? Charity begins at
home, is the voice of the world; yet it is every man
his greatest enemy, and, as it were, his own
executioner.

Thomas Browne

Superior people never make long visits.

Marianne Moore

One friend in a lifetime is much; two are many;
three are hardly possible.

Henry B. Adams

Cherishing children is the mark of a civilised society.

Joan Cooney

Someone asked where my roots were and I said, I hope in civilised behaviour.

Peter Ustinov

When a friend is in trouble, don't annoy him by asking if there is anything you can do. Think up something appropriate and do it.

E. W. Howe

Of all the icy blasts that blow on love, a request for money is the most chilling and havoc-wreaking.

Gustave Flaubert

Friendship is like earthenware, once broken it can be mended; love is like a mirror, once broken that ends it.

Josh Billings

Do not rely completely on any other human being. We meet all life's greatest tests alone.

Agnes MacPhail

Moral progress is the realisation that other human beings are fully as human as you are.

Philip Toynbee

If one sticks too rigidly to one's principles, one would hardly see anybody.

Agatha Christie

Friendship often ends in love, but love in friendship – never.

Charles Colton

Whatever people may say, the fastidious formal manner of the upper classes is preferable to the slovenly easygoing behaviour of the common middle classes. In moments of crisis, the former know how to act, the latter become uncouth brutes.

Cesare Pavese

Friendships begun in this world will be taken up again, never to be broken off.

Francis de Sales

Nothing is ever lost by courtesy. It is the cheapest
of the pleasures; costs nothing and conveys much.
It pleases him who gives and him who receives,
and thus, like mercy, it is twice blessed.

Erastius Wiman

You see someone on the street and essentially
what you notice about them is the flaw.

Diane Arbus

Friendships are fragile and precious things, and
require as careful handling as any other fragile and
precious thing.

Randolph Bourne

No distance of place or lapse of time can lessen the
friendship of those who are thoroughly persuaded
of each other's worth.

Robert Southey

A friend is someone who sees through you and
still enjoys the view.

Wilma Askinas

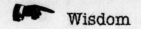

Before doing someone a favour, make sure that he isn't a madman.

Eugene Labiche

We can live without our friends but not without our neighbours.

Thomas Fuller

We deliberately waste time only with those we love – it is the purest sign that we love someone if we choose to spend time idly in their presence when we could be doing something more productive.

Sheila Cassidy

Distrust all those who love you extremely upon a very slight acquaintance and without any visible reason.

Lord Chesterfield

True friendship is like sound health: the value of it is seldom known until it is lost.

Charles Colton

Friend is sometimes a word devoid of meaning; enemy never.

Victor Hugo

The worst people in the world are the richest and the poorest.

William C. Hunter

Each departed friend is a magnet that attracts us to the next world.

Jean Paul Richter

The ornaments of a house are the friends who frequent it.

Ralph Waldo Emerson

The loss of a friend is like that of a limb; time may heal the anguish of the wound, but the loss cannot be repaired.

Robert Southey

The institution of monarchy in any form is an insult to the human race.

Mark Twain

Don't walk in front of me, I may not follow; don't walk behind me, I may not lead; walk beside me, and just be my friend.

Albert Camus

There is one thing that keeps surprising you about stormy old friends after they die – their silence.

Ben Hecht

Most people commit the same mistake with God as they make with their friends – they do all the talking.

Fulton J. Sheen

A society made up of individuals who were all capable of original thought would probably be unendurable. The pressure of ideas would simply drive it frantic.

H. L. Mencken

I believe sexuality is the basis if all friendship.

Jean Cocteau

Friendship and Society

The Social Contract is nothing more or less than a vast conspiracy of human beings to lie to and humbug one another for the general Good. Lies are the mortar that bind the savage individual into the social masonry.

H. G. Wells

He who has a thousand friends has not a friend to spare.
And he who has one enemy will meet him everywhere.

Ali Ibn-Abit-Talib

The friendship that can cease has never been real.

St Jerome

The love of our neighbour is the only door out of the dungeon of self.

George MacDonald

What will people say? In these words lies the tyranny of the world, the whole destruction of our natural disposition, the oblique vision of our minds.

Auerbach

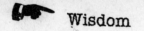

A home-made friend wears longer than one you buy in the market.

Austin O'Malley

Sharing food with another human being is an intimate act that should not be indulged in lightly.

M. F. K. Fisher

All you will get from strangers is surface pleasantry or indifference. Only someone who loves you will criticise you.

Judith Crist

So long as we are loved by others I should say that we are almost indispensable; and no man is useless while he has a friend.

Robert Louis Stevenson

The best way to keep your friends is not to give them away.

Wilson Mizner

What is a friend? A single soul dwelling in two bodies.

Aristotle

Property is not theft, but a good deal of theft
becomes property.

R. H. Tawney

I love you, and because I love you, I would sooner
have you hate me for telling the truth than adore
me for telling you lies.

Pietro Aretino

The freedom of any society varies proportionately
with the volume of its laughter.

Zero Mostel

One can drown in compassion if one answers
every call. It's another way of suicide.

Patrick White

If you have no enemies, you are apt to be in the
same predicament with regard to friends.

Elbert Hubbard

Enemies publish themselves. They declare war. The
friend never declares his love.

Henry D. Thoreau

The glory of friendship is not the outstretched hand, nor the kindly smile nor the joy of companionship; it is the spiritual inspiration that comes to one when he discovers that someone else believes in him and is willing to trust him.

Ralph Waldo Emerson

If you cannot mould yourself as you would wish, how can you expect other people to be entirely to your liking?

Thomas à Kempis

If you would keep a secret from an enemy, do not tell it to a friend.

Benjamin Franklin

Even the best of friends cannot attend each other's funeral.

Stephen Covey

A true friend is one who likes you despite your achievements.

Arnold Bennett

A good friend is one who tells you your faults in private.

Ken Alstad

It is well that there is no one without a fault, for he would not have a friend in the world. He would seem to belong to a different species.

William Hazlitt

I destroy my enemies when I make them my friends.

Abraham Lincoln

A true friend is one who overlooks your failures and tolerates your successes.

Doug Larson

Everybody's friend is nobody's.

Arthur Schopenhauer

No friendship is so cordial or delicious as that of a girl for a girl; no hatred so intense and immovable as that of woman for woman.

Walter Savage Landor

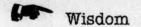

One of the most difficult things to give away is kindess – it is usually returned.

Gerald Owens

Successful people are always looking for opportunities to help others. Unsuccessful people are always asking, 'What's in it for me?'

Brian Tracy

Never forget where you came from; some day you might have to go back.

Cynthia Barnes

Miscellaneous

Beauty is the purgation of superfluities.

Michelangelo

The best screen actor is one who can do nothing supremely well.

Alfred Hitchcock

The notion of making money by popular work, and then retiring to do good work on the proceeds, is the most familiar of all the devil's traps for artists.

Logan Pearsall Smith

Sleep, riches, and health, to be truly enjoyed must be interrupted.

Jean Paul Richter

We think caged birds sing, when indeed they cry.

John Webster

Nothing is so wonderful when you get used to it.

E. W. Howe

Nothing is more responsible for the good old days than a bad memory.

Franklin P. Adams

Artists must be sacrificed to their art. Like bees, they must put their lives into the sting they give.

Ralph Waldo Emerson

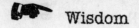

We can't all be heroes because somebody has to sit on the kerb and clap as they go by.

Will Rogers

The courage of the poet is to keep ajar the door that leads into madness.

Christopher Morley

A vigorous five-mile walk will do more good for an unhappy but otherwise healthy adult than all the medicine and psychology in the world.

Dudley White

When the oak is felled the whole forest echoes with its fall, but a hundred acorns are downed in silence by an unnoticed breeze.

Thomas Carlyle

It isn't the mountain ahead that wears you out – it's the grain in your shoe.

Robert Service

That virgin, vital, fine day: today.

Stéphane Mallarmé

Miscellaneous

Life's best balm is forgetfulness.

Felicia Hemans

Illness is the night-side of life, a more onerous citizenship. Everyone who is born holds dual citizenship, in the kingdom of the well and in the kingdom of the sick.

Susan Sontag

Hunger is not debatable.

Harry Hopkins

Nothing happens to you that hasn't happened to someone else.

William Feather

A medical maxim – when you hear hoofbeats, think of horses before zebras.

Harley Smith

It is unfulfilled dreams that keep you alive.

Robert Schuller

Our worst enemies are not the simple and the ignorant however cruel; our worst enemies are the corrupt and the intelligent.

Graham Greene

It is not the employer who pays the wages – he only handles the money. It is the product that pays wages.

Henry Ford

We must leave no Giotto among the hill shepherds.

John Ruskin

Popularity? It is glory's small change.

Victor Hugo

A burden in the bush is worth two on your hands.

James Thurber

One sees great things from the valley, only small things from the peak.

G. K. Chesterton

There is nothing ugly; I never saw an ugly thing in my life: for let the form of an object be what it may – light, shade and perspective will always make it beautiful.

John Constable

I give you bitter pills in sugar coating. The pills are harmless: the poison is in the sugar.

Stanislaw Lec

The only sure thing about luck is that it will change.

Bret Harte

You can't get rid of poverty by giving people money.

P. J. O'Rourke

The only thing one can be proud of is of having worked in such a way that an official reward for your labour cannot be envisaged by anyone.

Jean Cocteau

Rewards of any kind are but vulgarity.

R. B. Graham

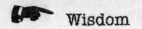

Toothache doesn't stop hurting just because someone has cancer.

Andrea Newman

The child was diseased at birth-stricken with an hereditary ill that only the most vital men are able to shake off. I mean poverty – the most deadly and prevalent of all diseases.

Eugene O'Neill

The most anxious man in the prison is the governor.

George Bernard Shaw

Anybody who has ever struggled with poverty knows how extremely expensive it is to be poor.

James Baldwin

Love is like any other luxury. You have no right to it unless you can afford it.

Anthony Trollope

Professional critics are those who brush the clothes of their betters.

Francis Bacon

Is there anything in life so disenchanting as attainment?

> Robert Louis Stevenson

If you have only a hammer, you tend to see every problem as a nail.

> Abraham Maslow

In America, through pressure of conformity, there is freedom of choice, but nothing to choose from.

> Peter Ustinov

A great city is one that handles art and garbage equally well.

> Bob Talbert

The whole difference between construction and creation is exactly this: that a thing constructed can be loved only after it is constructed; but a thing created is loved before it exists.

> G. K. Chesterton

The receptionist is by definition underpaid to lie.

> Karen Brodine

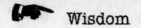

Mental health problems do not affect three or four out of every five persons, but one out of one.

William Menninger

Insanity in individuals is rare – but in groups, parties, nations and epochs, it is the rule.

Friedrich Nietzsche

Travel is ninety per cent anticipation and ten per cent recollection.

Edward Streeter

You will never 'find' time for anything. If you want time you must make it.

Charles Buxton

The real enemies of society are sitting snug behind typewriters and microphones pursuing their work of destruction amid popular applause.

Evelyn Waugh

Nothing is more unpleasant than a virtuous person with a mean mind.

Walter Bagehot

Man is not a balloon going up into the sky, nor a mole burrowing merely in the earth; but rather a thing like a tree, whose roots are fed from the earth, while its highest branches seem to rise almost to the stars.

G. K. Chesterton

What difference does it make to the dead, the orphans and the homeless, whether the mad destruction is wrought under the name of totalitarianism or the holy name of liberty and democracy?

Mahatma Gandhi

The only history that is worth a tinker's damn is the history we make today.

Henry Ford

By increasing the size of the keyhole, today's playwrights are in danger of doing away with the door.

Peter Ustinov

Wealth makes everything easy – honesty most of all.

Marie de Beausacq

Money and sex are forces too unruly for our reason; they can be controlled only by taboos which we tamper with at our peril.

Logan Pearsall Smith

In most betting shops you will see three windows marked 'Bet here' but only one window with the legend 'Pay Out'.

Jeffrey Bernard

The flavour of frying bacon beats orange blossom.

E. W. Howe

Many a gentle mind dwells in a deformed tabernacle.

Edmund Spencer

The ultimate result of shielding men from the effects of folly is to fill the world with fools.

Herbert Spencer

Nothing is truer than a funeral oration. It tells precisely what the dead man should have been.

J. Vaperean

Sometime the road is less travelled for a reason.

Desmond Cleary

There is a rage to organise which is the sworn
enemy of order.

Georges Duhamel

As long as a word remains unspoken, you are its
master; once you utter it, you are its slave.

Solomon Ibn Gabirol

As a white candle in a holy place,
so is the beauty of an aged face.

Joseph Campbell

Find something that isn't a miracle, you'll have
cause to wonder then.

Laurence Housman

The part never calls for nudity, and I've never used
that excuse. The box office calls for it.

Helen Mirren

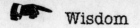

Anyone remotely interesting is mad, in some way or other.

John Green

A room without books is like a body without a soul.

Cicero

One of the best reasons for remaining at the bottom is simply to look at the men at the top.

Frank Moore Colby

Bookshops are centres of civilisation.

Rebecca West

The pistol is the sceptre of the bully.

George Meredith

Chess is a game of bloodless sadism and schemed execution.

Frederic Raphael

I decline utterly to be impartial as between the fire brigade and the fire.

Winston Churchill

Language has created the word loneliness to express the pain of being alone, and the word solitude to express the glory of being alone.

Paul Tillich

Preservation of health is a duty.

Herbert Spencer

There is more credit and satisfaction in being a first-rate truck driver than a tenth-rate executive.

C. Forbes

Give us this day our television, and an automobile, but deliver us from freedom.

Jean-Luc Godard

The quality of a person's life is in direct proportion to their commitment to excellence, regardless of their chosen field of endeavour.

Vince Lombardi

Everybody has his own theatre, in which he is manager, actor, prompter, playwright, scene-shifter, boxkeeper, doorkeeper, all in one, and audience into the bargain.

Julius Hare

Wisdom

Performers and their public should never meet. Once the curtain comes down, the performer should fly away like the magician's dove.

Edith Piaf

Things you possess in too great abundance belong not to you but to the poor.

Christine de Pisan

You have power over people only as long as you don't take everything away from them. But when you have robbed a man of everything he's no longer in your power – he's free again.

Alexander Solzhenitsyn

If you board the wrong train, it is no use running along the corridor in the opposite direction.

Dietrich Bonhoeffer

It takes 15,000 casualties to train a major-general.

Marshal Foch

There is a hook in every benefit, that sticks in his jaws that takes the benefit, and draws him whither the benefactor will.

John Donne

He is a barbarian and thinks that the customs of his tribe and island are the laws of nature.

George Bernard Shaw

Without the divine drop of oil we call humour the great world machine would soon grind to a standstill.

Hugo Rahner

Fear is tragedy played at a thousand revolutions per minute.

John Mortimer

I succeed Benjamin Franklin; no one can replace him.

Thomas Jefferson

A man who cannot tolerate small ills can never accomplish great things.

Lin Yutang

Genius is perseverance in disguise.

Mike Newline

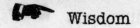

Fortune is a great deceiver. She sells very dear the things she seems to give us.

Vincent Voiture

The rung of a ladder was never meant to rest upon, but only to hold a man's foot long enough to enable him to put the other somewhat higher.

T. H. Huxley

Handel is the greatest composer who has ever lived. I would uncover my head and kneel at his grave.

Ludwig van Beethoven

The worst evil of being in prison is that one can never bar one's door.

Henri Beyle

Children watch too much television not only because indolent parents allow them to, but because the standard of most programmes is pitched at their level.

Richard Ingrams

There are people who have money and there are people who are rich.

Coco Chanel

Electric light is a most efficient policeman and rain is the best policeman of all.

Louis D. Brandeis

Life is a moderately good play with a badly-written third act.

Truman Capote

Index

LITS2